D0658411

THE CONSCIOUS PARENT'S
GUIDE TO

Raising
Boys

THE CONSCIOUS PARENT'S GUIDE TO

Raising Boys

ENCOURAGE POSITIVE COMMUNICATION

A mindful approach to raising a confident, resilient son

STRENGTHEN YOUR RELATIONSHIP

PROMOTE SELF-ESTEEM

Cheryl L. Erwin, MA, LMFT, AND Jennifer Costa

Adams Media
New York London Toronto Sydney New Delhi

Adams Media
An Imprint of Simon & Schuster, Inc.
57 Littlefield Street
Avon, Massachusetts 02322
Copyright © 2017 by Simon & Schuster, Inc.

ADAMS MEDIA and colophon are trademarks of Simon and Schuster.

For information about special discounts for bulk purchases, please contact Simon & Schuster Special Sales at 1-866-506-1949 or business@simonandschuster.com.

The Simon & Schuster Speakers Bureau can bring authors to your live event. For more information or to book an event contact the Simon & Schuster Speakers Bureau at 1-866-248-3049 or visit our website at www.simonspeakers.com.

Manufactured in the United States of America

10 9 8 7 6 5 4 3 2

Library of Congress Cataloging-in-Publication Data has been applied for.

ISBN 978-1-4405-9994-1
ISBN 979-1-4405-9995-8 (ebook)

This book is intended as general information only, and should not be used to diagnose or treat any health condition. In light of the complex, individual, and specific nature of health problems, this book is not intended to replace professional medical advice. The ideas, procedures, and suggestions in this book are intended to supplement, not replace, the advice of a trained medical professional. Consult your physician before adopting any of the suggestions in this book, as well as about any condition that may require diagnosis or medical attention. The author and publisher disclaim any liability arising directly or indirectly from the use of this book.

Many of the designations used by manufacturers and sellers to distinguish their products are claimed as trademarks. Where those designations appear in this book and Simon & Schuster, Inc., was aware of a trademark claim, the designations have been printed with initial capital letters.

Contains material adapted from *The Everything® Parent's Guide to Raising Boys, 2nd Edition* by Cheryl L. Erwin, MA, MFT, copyright © 2011 by Simon & Schuster, Inc., ISBN 13: 978-1-4405-0689-5.

Contents

Introduction

Being a conscious parent involves more that just being a caregiver to your son. It is a nurturing and educational process that allows you to forge strong bonds with your boy and help him grow from a helpless infant to an independent, self-reliant adult.

Few things in life are as important as raising a child. You may have dreamt of the birth of your baby, read stacks of books and magazine articles, attended classes, and talked eagerly with other parents. Then your baby—a real, flesh-and-blood boy—arrives. Suddenly nothing is as clear and simple as it once seemed.

The realities of raising a boy take even the most loving, committed, educated parents by surprise. At first, the challenges are fairly straightforward: You want him to eat, sleep, and, occasionally, give you a moment's peace. Soon he develops a personality of his own. He finds interesting new ways to explore his world. And sometimes he proves not to be exactly what (or who) you expected.

In addition to understanding just how your son's gender affects his development and behavior, you must learn how to connect with him on an emotional level so that you can make mindful choices regarding his upbringing. Boys learn differently than girls and have different strengths; they sometimes need different things from parents.

No one will ever know your boy like you do. You must decide what you want for your son and be willing to follow through every day of your lives together. You most certainly love your son, but love is not always enough to raise a kind and well-adjusted man. You must learn to mix love with wisdom, good judgment, understanding, and self-control. Conscious parents learn to rely on both their heads and their hearts, ask for help when they need it, and are willing to learn from their own mistakes.

The Conscious Parent's Guide to Raising Boys offers you information and suggestions and can—with your own wisdom and experience—help you raise a successful, capable, and happy young man.

 **CHAPTER 1**

Conscious Parenting

Being a conscious parent is based on building strong, sustainable bonds with your children through mindful living and awareness. Traditional power-based parenting techniques that promote compliance and obedience can disconnect you from your children. Conscious parenting, on the other hand, helps you develop a positive emotional connection with your child. You acknowledge your child's unique self and attempt to empathize with his way of viewing the world. Through empathetic understanding and tolerance you create a safe environment where your child feels that his ideas and concerns are truly being heard. When you find yourself in a stressful situation with your child, rather than reacting with anger or sarcasm, conscious parenting reminds you to instead take a step back, reflect, and find a peaceful solution—one that honors your child's individuality and motivations. This approach benefits all children, especially boys. There are some distinct biological differences between boys and girls that affect their behavior and development, and understanding just how his gender impacts the choices that your child makes can help you to be an effective parent. Adopting the conscious parenting philosophy can relieve your stress and improve your child's self-image. The strong bond built between you and your child, along with your own calm, respectful attitude, helps him to develop positive behavior patterns.

The Benefits of Conscious Parenting

Conscious parenting isn't a set of rules or regulations that you must follow, but rather it is a system of beliefs. Conscious parents engage and connect with their children, using mindful and positive discipline rather than punishment. They try to be present when they're spending time with their children, avoiding distractions like TV and social media. Conscious parents respect their children and accept them as they are. The most important part of conscious parenting is building an emotional connection with your child so you can understand the underlying reasons for his behavior.

> Conscious parenting is about listening with full attention, and embracing a nonjudgmental acceptance of yourself and your child. As you engage in the act of *becoming*, you will discover a heightened sense of emotional awareness of yourself and your child, a clearer self-regulation in the parenting relationship, and a greater compassion for yourself and your child.

Conscious parenting brings with it a number of benefits, including improved communication, stronger relationships, and the feeling of greater happiness and satisfaction with life. Some of these benefits appear more immediately, while others take some time to emerge. The benefits of conscious parenting and mindfulness are a result of making it a part of your daily life. With practice, conscious parenting becomes an integral part of who and how you are in the world, and will in turn become a central part of who your child is as well.

WELL-BEING

Conscious parents understand that everything they do and say over the course of each day *matters*. It is a sense of the *now*, being in the present without regard or worry for the past or future. When you become more mindful, you may find that you become more accepting of the things in life that you can't change and experience less stress. The net result is greater satisfaction with and enjoyment of whatever each day has to offer. This sense of well-being offers a satisfaction and contentment in knowing that we are who we are intended to be, doing precisely what we are designed for in the moment.

> As human beings, we each possess the tools for contributing something of value. Assess your gifts and talents—those personality traits and skills that make you unique—and determine how to employ them to enhance your parenting. If you take a full accounting of yourself—good, bad, and indifferent—and *own* the sum total of your individual experience, you are taking the first step toward conscious parenting.

EMPATHY

The awareness you gain as a conscious parent has the practical purpose of redefining your perception of yourself and your compassionate understanding of your child. When you understand how your child experiences the world and how he learns, you can communicate in ways that really reach him. This largely happens through modeling, or teaching through example. Doing so allows you to pass on the values and lessons that are important to you, regardless of your beliefs. Having an awareness of how your son's gender influences his behavior will only help you to appreciate the world from his point of view.

ACCEPTANCE AND VALIDATION

Your child relies upon you and your family to provide a solid foundation of self-esteem. Equipped with a strong sense of self-worth, your child will be better prepared to enter into a life that will likely present many challenges. Much of your time and energy will be expended on raising, counseling, and disciplining your child in ways that he will understand. It is also important for you to reinforce your love and appreciation of his gifts and talents.

Are Boys Different from Girls?

Psychologist Elaine Aron, PhD, tells the story of an informal experiment regarding gender. A young infant was left in a park with an attendant who claimed to have agreed to sit with the baby for a few minutes, not knowing if it was a boy or a girl. Many people stopped to admire the infant, and every one of them was upset about not knowing the baby's gender. Several even volunteered to undress the baby to find out.

Gender turns out to be one of the earliest expectations parents have for their children. Some parents pray for a son; others hope for a daughter. Why? Are boys and girls really that different?

Until recently, even researchers were reluctant to talk much about gender differences. In the world of women's liberation and political correctness, there was something suspicious about saying that girls and boys might be inherently different. Parents were encouraged to avoid gender bias and were discouraged from teaching stereotypes to their sons and daughters. Little girls should not be restricted to dolls, this reasoning went; instead, they should be encouraged to become police officers and doctors, not "just mommies."

Little boys faced an even more difficult challenge. You may agree that it is good for girls to explore their strengths, but is it really all right for boys to explore their sensitivities? The same parent who chuckles as his son tumbles around the playground, shaking his head and saying with a smile, "Boys will be boys," may feel a small stab of worry when that same little boy picks up his sister's doll and contentedly settles down to play.

Much of what you have learned about boys and girls comes from generations of assumptions, your own parents, your friends, and the world around you. For example, you may believe that boys are strong while girls are weaker. Boys are brave; girls are more timid. Girls are allowed to cry; boys had better not cry in public.

Researchers Rebecca Parlakian and Claire Lerner found that parents of toddlers react more positively to children in gender-traditional play, such as girls playing with dolls, and more negatively to children engaged in nontraditional play, such as boys playing with dolls. This undoubtedly reflects cultural beliefs about gender roles and shows how early these beliefs are communicated to children.

Society allows girls to be giddy and silly; boys must demonstrate that they know how to be manly. Even in this liberated world, working women still bear the bulk of the responsibility for childcare, keeping a home, cooking, and cleaning. Why? Well, our culture still assumes that those jobs are women's work. Many mothers never train their sons to do these tasks.

As you hold your own precious son in your arms or watch him begin to explore the world around him, you may find yourself wondering exactly what it means to raise a son. What is masculinity, anyway? What do you need to know to raise a healthy, happy boy, one who grows up to be a healthy, happy man?

Conscious Parenting and Boys

Your son's gender is just one of the many traits that make up his personality. Making an effort to explore each of these unique traits, including his gender, will help you to relate to him on a deeper level.

The extent to which your son's gender influences his personality and behaviors will vary, based on quite a few factors. For example, two children may share a common interest in basketball. They both spend time playing the game and thinking about it. The first boy grows up with an appreciation for the game, which influences his decision to become a physical education teacher, and he later ends up coaching his local middle school team. The second boy dedicates himself to building his skills as a basketball player. Also influenced by his love of the game, he accepts a basketball scholarship from a university and graduates with a degree in communications, later becoming a sports writer. Both boys had something in common. How this commonality influenced their life paths was based on their unique personalities and a myriad of outside factors.

Think of the traits that make your child unique. Does he have a particular interest or ability that stands out? Your child's individual gifts and experiences make up his whole self. Gender is just one of the many factors to consider when making parenting decisions regarding your child.

Your appreciation of your child's uniqueness will make your home and family a place where he is unconditionally loved and understood. Many parents of boys have successfully implemented the conscious parenting philosophy in their family lives, and it has had a tremendous effect on their son's happiness.

WHAT IS A TYPICAL BOY?

Take a moment to think: Suppose someone asked you to describe a typical boy. What would you say? You might describe a rough-and-tumble kid who loves to run and climb, play baseball or soccer, and get dirty building fortresses in the backyard. You might describe a young person who is courteous, respectful, kind, reliable, strong, and able to take care of himself—at least most of the time. You might talk about a boy with holes in the knees of his jeans, untied shoelaces, and a face smeared with jelly, one with worms in his pockets and a reluctance to show weakness. Perhaps your typical boy would be stoic, courageous in the face of danger, and fearless when faced with a challenge.

But is that an accurate description of a real boy? More importantly, is it an accurate description of your own son? Sometimes flesh-and-blood boys don't match their parents' expectations, with consequences that are troubling for everyone.

Exploring Your Own Expectations

What you believe about boys in general and your own son in particular will have a powerful influence on the child, the young man, and the adult he becomes. As his parent, you shape the world your son inhabits, teaching him by your example about the things that truly matter in life. You will teach him—often without realizing you are doing so—about men, women, love, life, and success. Your son will begin his life by seeing himself through your eyes. If you're thinking that this is a heavy responsibility, you're correct.

What if you want very much for your son to follow in your footsteps, but he refuses? People generally respond better to invitations than they do to commands. You can teach your son about what you enjoy and share it with him, but you cannot force him to become something he is not. He will be healthiest and happiest when he is free to explore his own path—with your guidance and support.

All parents have hopes and dreams for their children; you will, too. But part of being a mindful and loving parent is balancing your own expectations for your son with a realistic understanding of who your son truly is—heart and soul.

Think for a moment about your own childhood. What was the mood in the home you grew up in? Did you feel good enough just as you were, or were your parents critical and demanding? What do you think your parents believed about your siblings? Were you loved more, or less? Did you feel a sense of belonging and worth, or did you constantly have to work harder to earn your parents' approval? What impact do you think your childhood has had on your adult life?

All children are born hardwired to connect to their parents, and all children crave their parents' love, approval, and support. As the years pass, you will undoubtedly discover that your son's task in life is to become himself. He will match your expectations in some ways and surprise you in many others.

What Do You Want for Your Son?

Imagine for a moment that someone has handed you the keys to a beautiful, high-powered new car. Let's say that you don't check the tires, the gas, or the oil. You don't decide on a destination or get out a map. You don't pack a lunch or water to drink. You just jump behind the wheel, turn on the ignition, and stomp on the accelerator. What do you suppose will happen?

Sometimes parents approach raising a child just that impulsively; each day becomes its own crisis. You must help your son to sleep through the night, crawl, walk, use the toilet, and, eventually, go off to school. He must learn to do his homework and his chores, drive, and come home on time. It can be tempting to look no further ahead than today's challenges, and there will certainly be many of those as you parent your growing boy. Short-range parenting may work for today, but it may not be the best approach for your son's long-range health and happiness—or yours.

LONG-RANGE PARENTING

Here's a suggestion: Imagine that thirty years have gone by and your son is now an adult. What sort of life do you want him to have? What character qualities are important to you? What skills do you believe he will need to be successful? When he is grown, what kind of man do you want him to be? Take the time to sit down with your son's other parent, or on your own if you are single, and write down the answers to these questions. Most parents discover that they have never really thought about parenting in this way before.

You may find that you want your son to be responsible, compassionate, confident, and kind. You may want him to be successful, educated, spiritual, and independent. You may wish for him to have stable relationships, a happy marriage, and healthy children of his own someday.

ROOTS AND WINGS

Post your list of skills and character qualities that you want your son to develop where you will see it often. Then, as you and your son travel through life together, use your list as a map to your final destination. The spilled juice, the temper tantrum, and the chores left undone—all are opportunities to learn and to teach your son what he needs to know to be successful and to build a relationship that will last both of you a lifetime.

A wise person once said that a parent's job is to give a child both roots and wings—roots so they always know that they can return home for love and comfort, and wings so they can soar. Learning to know the fascinating person your boy really is will help you give him the foundation and the joy he needs to soar through life.

Important Points to Consider

There are some distinct differences between raising boys and raising girls. As you develop a conscious parenting plan for your son, consider the following points:

- Gender is just one of the many characteristics that make your son unique. If an approach works well for one child, it might not necessarily be a good fit for another.

- Boys need love, touch, and unconditional support from their parents, just as girls do.

- Consider your own expectations for raising a boy and take the time to write out a document that outlines what you want for him.

 **CHAPTER 2**

Preparing Yourself for Parenting

Your son's journey toward adulthood is influenced by the traits and qualities he was born with, but it is also shaped by your personality, who you are, and what you bring to the process of parenting. As a parent, learning to be open and accepting of your son's unique self will help him grow with confidence—and there is no better way to do that than through conscious parenting.

Your Experiences Affect Your Child

How do we become who we are? Here's a simple explanation: A child is born with a certain set of traits and genetic tendencies. He may be short or tall, blond or dark-haired; he may have physical strength and coordination or an inborn gift for music and creativity. He may be naturally optimistic or a bit negative. He will have to use the abilities he was born with to make sense of his surroundings, and to decide how to thrive—or how to survive.

Humans have a need to attach meaning to everything they experience. We create meaning—in other words, we make unconscious decisions—about everything in our lives, from whether or not we're loved and wanted to whether we're smart or cute or athletic. Researchers call these early decisions *adaptations* and say that they make up much of our adult personalities. Not surprisingly, parents have a significant impact on the adaptations their children make.

The experiences you encountered and the decisions you made growing up have shaped the way your brain responds to relationships—including your relationship with your son. Exploring, understanding, and accepting your childhood experiences will help you understand and connect with your son as he grows.

One of the most valuable things you can do as a parent is to spend time understanding your own experiences and what you have decided about yourself and others as a result. Daniel J. Siegel, MD, and Mary Hartzell, MEd, suggest some questions to ponder in their thought-provoking look at neurobiology and parenting, *Parenting from the Inside Out*. Take a moment to think about these questions and write down your answers.

O Who was in your family when you were growing up?

O What was your relationship with your mother like? Your father? Do you ever try to be like (or different from) one of your parents?

○ How did your parents discipline you? How do you feel that affects your role as a parent now?

○ How did your parents communicate with you when you were happy and excited? When you were angry or unhappy, what would happen? Did your father and mother respond differently to you during emotional times? How?

○ What impact do you think your childhood has had on your adult life in general, including the way you think of yourself as a parent and the way you relate to your own children? If you could change something about the way you relate to your son, what would it be?

You may not think your own attitude and experiences have anything to do with how you raise your son, but the fascinating field of attachment parenting teaches us otherwise. Parents who have come to terms with their own past and who feel confident about their ability to raise a child, and their child's ability to grow into a good person, are better prepared to have healthy parental relationships.

LEARN FROM YOUR PAST

Your answer to the questions about your childhood probably stirred up some old memories. Perhaps some were happy; others may have made you feel sad or even angry. Take the time to reflect on your memories and notice whether or not it's easy to tell your own story. If you can start at the beginning of your life and relate your autobiography smoothly, without large gaps, and without feelings of trauma or distress, chances are that you have a coherent narrative.

Stories—our own and those of others—are how we make sense of our lives. Researchers tell us that what happens to us is not as important as what we decide about what happens to us. In other words, the meaning you have attached to your early experience, and if you have learned to accept your unique self, is more important than the facts of what happened to you.

Your parents influenced your early experiences, for better or worse. You are now influencing your son's. Taking the time to understand where you came from (and decide where you want to go) will help you be an understanding and caring parent.

The Power of Attachment

Not long ago, even experts believed that the human brain had a solitary existence within a single human skull. New technology, however, has allowed scientists to peer within the living brain, and what they have discovered is both exciting and sobering. Your brain is a highly social organ. It is designed to connect with other brains, and it literally changes its structure and function over your life span. The most powerful element in creating these changes is relationships with family, friends, and other significant people in your life.

> When children have a predictable and repeatable experience of being cared for, it creates what is called a *secure attachment*. Security gives children the sense of well-being necessary to explore their world and develop in healthy ways. Understanding yourself and creating a secure bond with your son is crucial for getting him off to a good start in life.

SECURE ATTACHMENT

About half of all people have a secure attachment. This means that they have enjoyed responsive care and communication with a parent or other caregiver and have felt supported at times of emotional stress. Other people have not been so fortunate. Their parents were not able to offer them a secure attachment, and their ability to have strong, healthy relationships was affected.

As Siegel and Hartzell point out in *Parenting from the Inside Out*, how you respond to your son's emotions is vital. Imagine that your excited little boy brings you a beetle. You might say, "Wow, look at how green his wings are! Thank you for showing him to me." Or you might say, "Get that thing out of the house right now!" Your responses over time will help determine how connected and understood your son feels with you.

BUILDING ATTACHMENT

You may have had a secure attachment with your own parents and now find it easy to be perceptive, supportive, and responsive with your son (at least most of the time). Research tells us, however, that when a parent is unwilling or unable to respond to a child consistently, the child will adapt by avoiding closeness to the parent, or by becoming anxious about the relationship.

> Children who were abused or neglected often fail to develop the ability to reason well, regulate emotions, or connect well with others. Attachment, it turns out, is a powerful predictor of the relationships we have later in life.

Parents who had an insecure attachment to their own parents are often emotionally unavailable, unresponsive, overly intrusive, or rejecting with their own children. They may lack empathy and find it difficult to deal with their children's emotions or to offer love and nurturing. The good news, however, is that we are not doomed to repeat mistakes made in the past.

Here are some suggestions for building a secure attachment with your infant son:

O Understand that each baby is truly unique. Some babies are calm and mellow; others are fussy. Avoid the temptation to compare your son with other babies; learn his individual mannerisms and cues.

O Pay close attention to your son's facial expressions, body movements, and noises. They provide clues to understanding what he needs, including his signals for sleep or food.

O Be sensitive to your son's response to touch and physical pressure so you understand how to hold him in a way that invites closeness and trust.

○ Talk, laugh, and play with your baby boy often, and when you do, give him your complete attention. No, you might not get all the household chores done, but you are building a lifelong relationship with your son.

Remember that understanding and interpreting your baby's movements and signals will get easier with practice and familiarity.

Finding Balance

Your son deserves the best you can give him. He needs your time, energy, commitment, patience, and love. But take a moment to think: If you always put yourself last on your list of priorities, what will happen to your own physical, spiritual, and emotional health? What will your son decide about his place in the world? About you? The long-term results of always putting your son first and neglecting your own needs may not be what you intend—or what you want. After all, conscious parenting is about being aware of not just your child's needs but your own as well. As any grounded parent knows, you must take care of yourself in order to be truly present for your child.

CARING FOR YOURSELF

Remember, your son is watching you constantly for clues about what matters most in life. He will learn to respect you when you respect yourself; he will learn to value and appreciate life when you show him how. And he will learn to be demanding and self-centered if your actions teach him that he should always get what he wants the moment he wants it. Raising a healthy son requires that you be a healthy parent.

Keep Yourself Physically Healthy

Exercise is a powerful antidepressant and antianxiety remedy; it also strengthens your heart and mind. Take time on a regular basis to attend a yoga class, go for a run, play a sport, or take a vigorous walk with a friend. Eat a healthy diet and do your best to get enough sleep. You will have more energy and patience (and less illness) if you take care of your body.

Keep Yourself Mentally Alert

More than one parent of a young child has found himself cutting a friend's meat at dinner or babbling about toilet training. Don't forget to be a grownup on occasion. You can take a class once a week, take time to read a good book, or enjoy other stimulating activities. (No, it isn't selfish, and it won't harm your son.) You will tolerate the routines and repetition of parenting far better when you have something of your own to look forward to.

Keep Yourself Emotionally Connected

As much as you undoubtedly love your son, you are still an adult, and you need adult support and connection. Do your best to make time for your friendships; a telephone call to a friend can help you through the most difficult moments of life with a little one. Get together with other parents of children your son's age and share stories and experiences. It helps a great deal to know you're not alone.

Keep Yourself Spiritually Strong

You may find strength and comfort in church, synagogue, mosque, or other place of worship, or you may nurture yourself spiritually with work for the environment or a cause you believe in. Whatever it is that you are passionate about, be sure you make time for it in your daily life. Your son will learn best from your example, and the values you cherish can be something you share for a lifetime.

WISDOM, NOT SELFISHNESS

You may believe it is selfish to do things for yourself when you are a parent, and it is true that spending time with your son and time as a family are important. But taking care of yourself is not selfishness; it is wisdom. Imagine that the energy you possess is like water in a crystal pitcher. Every time you do something for someone else, deal with a crisis, or make a decision, you pour water out of your pitcher. What will happen when the pitcher is empty? Finding ways to keep your own pitcher full—by taking time to be physically, mentally, and spiritually healthy—is one of the most important aspects of being a wise and loving parent.

Take Time for Your Relationship

If you are a single parent, you face your own joys and challenges. If you are parenting with a partner, however, you need to take a moment to consider the impact of parenthood on your relationship. You might think that having a child would bring a couple closer together. After all, there is the joy of birth and the delight parents share in watching their youngster grow, learn, and explore his world. But while that is all true, it isn't always easy.

John Gottman, PhD, of the University of Washington has spent years studying marriage. He has found that 40–70 percent of all couples experience stress, conflict, and a drop in satisfaction with their relationship when a baby comes home.

Why? Well, moms often provide most of the hands-on care for infants, including nursing the baby, walking the floor when he cries, and getting up several times during the night. A new mother may experience postpartum depression and may have little energy for fun with Dad. Fathers, on the other hand, often report feeling excluded by the mother-and-baby duo and may find other ways of occupying themselves while their child is young. Sometimes the patterns that form during a child's early years are difficult to change as that child grows. When their son leaves home for good, what will remain of his parents' relationship?

Researchers at Ohio State University have found that couples who had a good relationship with each other when their child was an infant, but who disagreed about parenting, were more likely to have a poor relationship by the time their child was three years old. How you and your partner decide to co-parent your son influences your relationship with each other.

Remember, children watch the people around them and make decisions about what it all means. What will your son decide as he watches your relationship with his other parent? Numerous studies have shown that the way parents resolve conflict, express affection, support each other, communicate, and handle their sexual relationship has a strong influence on their children.

Be sure to take time for your own relationship, have fun, and connect with your partner. Make time every day for affection, laughter, and conversation. Your son will be watching and learning from what he sees.

The Value of Self-Control

Part of being a conscious parent is learning the value of controlling your own words and behavior rather than attempting to control your children. Is it always this easy? Absolutely not. But thinking carefully about your own thoughts, feelings, and actions is an excellent place to begin in creating a strong, loving relationship with your son.

When you lose your temper (or when your son loses his), the part of your brain responsible for thinking and reasoning disconnects, leaving you with only physical sensation and emotion. No one can solve problems effectively when he is angry. Before you respond to a challenge from your son, take a moment to calm yourself down. Then think about the underlying cause of his behavior and what you can both learn from the experience.

You are your son's earliest and best teacher. What you believe about yourself, what you've decided about your own experiences, and how you manage your own behavior will have a powerful impact on your growing boy.

Important Points to Consider

Your experiences growing up will affect the way you parent your son. You are his model, so addressing your own views and behaviors is an important part of conscious parenting.

○ Developing a secure attachment early on will help you connect with your son and parent him more effectively.

○ Caring for yourself and ensuring that your physical, emotional, and spiritual needs are met is vital for appropriately caring for your son.

○ You are your son's best teacher, and the choices you make will deeply affect the person he becomes.

 **CHAPTER 3**

Mindfully Parenting Your Son

As a conscious parent you understand that taking the time to securely connect to your son is the key to raising a happy and secure boy. But how exactly do you accomplish this? Mindful parenting—being present for your child—allows him to create a strong attachment to you that will in turn make him feel confident in himself. Realistically it can be hard to be consistently mindful when you are surrounded by dirty diapers, piles of laundry, and a crying infant, but as long as you can find some way to connect with your son each day, you are forming a relationship that will benefit him in his future life.

Forming a Relationship

Most parents have lots and lots of questions. You may be wondering how to help your son sleep through the night, become toilet trained, or dress himself. You may have questions about chores, allowance, or homework. Or you may be wondering if organized sports are really a good idea, how much television your son should watch, or whether to allow him to play video games. You will learn more about these issues in the pages ahead, but long before you can address all the daily challenges of raising a boy, something very important has to happen. It's called a relationship.

BELONGING AND SIGNIFICANCE

Children learn about life in the context of their relationships, and their earliest relationships are major influencers. Regardless of their gender, appearance, and talents, all children need to know that they belong, that there is a place in their families just for them. Children need assurance that they are accepted unconditionally and loved in spite of their occasionally challenging behavior.

In fact, recent research tells us that the most important gift a parent can give a growing child is a sense of being loved and accepted unconditionally. Taking time to build a secure attachment is essential to raising a happy, healthy son. Sounds easy, doesn't it? But ask any parent of a cranky, defiant three-year-old and she will tell you that it isn't always as easy as it sounds.

Children also need to have a sense of their own significance—the knowledge that they have worth apart from what they do or achieve—and that the choices they make in life matter. Children who know they belong and that they matter in their families and their world are more likely to become capable, productive members of their communities.

There are many ways to help children develop a healthy sense of belonging and significance. Among them are encouragement, active listening, spending time together, effective and respectful discipline, and the teaching of character and life skills.

Connecting with Your Son

Several years ago, a group of doctors, psychologists, and other researchers began studying a troubling issue. The rates of both behavioral and emotional problems among American children and adolescents appeared to be rising, and no one could really explain why. After all, our material wealth and comforts were improving. Why would children be suffering more?

Many observers of American life in the twenty-first century have noticed that the pace of family life appears to be accelerating at an alarming rate. It is now common (and often necessary) for both mothers and fathers to work outside the home and for children to spend a large part of their early lives in childcare. Even when the family is at home together, there seems to be little time for real connection. Everyone has his own television, computer, and cell phone. There are household chores to do. Work follows parents home, while children have outside activities and piles of homework. Multitasking is fine, unless parenting becomes just another task on the list of things to do.

More than 8 percent of U.S. high school students suffer from clinical depression; U.S. children as a group report more anxiety today than did psychiatric patients in the 1950s; and about 21 percent of U.S. children ages nine to seventeen have a diagnosable mental or addictive disorder. These problems can stem from a lack of connection to significant adults.

WHY CONNECTION IS IMPORTANT

Researchers now say that the human brain is hardwired from birth for one specific task: to connect with other brains. If you're the parent of a baby boy, that means *you*. Allan N. Schore, PhD, of the David Geffen School of Medicine at UCLA puts it this way: "The idea is that we are born to form attachments, that our brains are physically wired to develop in tandem with another's, through emotional communication, beginning before words are spoken."

Simply put, your baby boy needs connection with you as much as he needs food, safety, and shelter. When you hold him, rock him, and gaze into his eyes, you are helping his brain develop the circuitry for relationships and future learning. Your son needs lots of tenderness, time, and attention from you to develop and grow.

CREATING CONTINGENT COMMUNICATION

Consider for a moment a familiar scenario: It's late afternoon; your baby has been taking his nap and is still in his crib. You are in the kitchen, getting ready for dinner and the evening ahead of you. Suddenly, you hear your baby crying. What do you do? Well, most parents instinctively head for the bedroom to find out what's going on. Perhaps your son just woke up and is eager to be picked up and cuddled. Perhaps he's hungry or wet. He may even have developed a fever while he was sleeping and is feeling miserable.

Your own parental instincts kick in when you hold and look at your baby, and while all parents get their signals crossed occasionally, most of the time you know just what to do. Attentive parents and their babies enjoy what researchers call contingent communication, which, as it turns out, may be the most important single building block in brain development and secure attachment, as well as one of the few parenting skills that occurs in all known cultures.

Suppose that something gets in the way of this process. Perhaps the television is on and you don't hear the baby crying at all. Or you're depressed and tired and just don't feel like walking all the way back to your son's room to see what's wrong. Maybe you think he's hungry when he's actually wet, or you miss the fact that he has a fever or a rash. In this case, the baby's immediate physical needs will not be met. This is not contingent communication. No parent is perfect; no matter how hard you try, you will get the message wrong from time to time. But as long as your son learns that you listen, you care, and you will do your best to respond to his needs, he will grow and thrive.

Because boys usually lag behind girls in the development of their emotional and social skills, it is vital that you take time to listen, touch, talk, and connect with your son. He needs a relationship with you in order to become a happy, productive young man.

Contingent communication means that a child's signal is received and understood and that a parent responds appropriately. When communication between parent and child is caring and connected, a child thrives and his relationship with his parents grows stronger. Listening and responding to your son are two of the most important things you can do for him.

Understanding the Roots of Behavior

Parents spend a great deal of time, energy, and resources attempting to shape and change their child's behavior. Many approaches to discipline, such as punishment, rewards, time-out, grounding, and taking away possessions or privileges, are attempts to control what a child does.

There is a more effective way, however. Children want connection; they need a sense of belonging and significance. No matter if it is positive or negative, there is an underlying reason why a child behaves the way that he does, just as there is a reason why you react the way you do. This reason may be hard to discover, but as a conscious parent, you will eventually learn how to get to the bottom of things.

BELIEFS BEHIND BEHAVIOR IN ACTION

To better understand the importance of uncovering the beliefs behind your son's behavior, imagine the following scenario. You are a busy mom who runs a business from your home and often must spend a great deal of time on the telephone. This is fine with you, but it does not always work out well for your four-year-old son. Like all little boys his age, your son wants a sense of belonging and connection with his mom, and when you're four years old and an only child, that means constant, undivided attention.

One morning the phone rings, and you settle down to talk to your client. Your son, who has been happily building a castle with his blocks, looks over at you and sighs. You can almost hear him thinking, *Not again*. But he knows just how to get your attention.

"Moo-o-m," he whines, tugging on your jeans. "I need some juice."

"Sshhh, honey, I'm on the phone," you whisper, and then say into the phone, "Hold on a moment; it's my little boy." You turn to him. "You know where the juice boxes are," you say impatiently. "Go ahead and get yourself one."

You return to your call, and your son wanders into the kitchen. He gets himself a juice box from the refrigerator but—uh-oh—manages to spill half of it putting the straw in the little hole. When you return to the kitchen and see the mess, your son gives you a "Who me?" look, puts the box down in the puddle of juice, and begins to draw designs on the kitchen floor in fruit punch.

Jane Nelsen, EdD, points out that children's behavior is a form of code. Their actions are their way of telling you what they think, feel, and need. Sometimes their behavior is misguided, but you will be a more effective parent when you look for the beliefs behind your child's behavior and work with him to solve the problems you face.

You can tell him to get a sponge, but the damage is done. If you remain on the phone, he will continue to invent new ways to attract your attention. He has learned during his four years that misbehavior will get your attention when good behavior does not. And having Mom mad at him feels more like connection to a four-year-old than being ignored.

DEALING WITH BELIEFS BEFORE BEHAVIOR

What should you do now? Misbehavior is an invitation to look for solutions. Your son seems to believe that he matters to you only when he has your undivided attention, and you will be most effective when you plan for these discouraging moments. Yelling, lecturing, or sending your son to a punitive time-out are unlikely to help. After considering the root of your son's behavior, lay out a plan. For example:

○ **Sit down with your son and let him know that you need to spend some time on the phone for business.** Remind him that your business allows you to be at home with him, which is important to you, and then ask for his help. (Children can be cooperative and creative when asked for their feedback and assistance, and they can be defiant when ordered to obey.)

○ **Ask your son if he has any ideas about what he could do when you have to make a phone call.** Perhaps you could make a "phone bag" full of inexpensive small toys and books to be used only when you are on the phone.

○ **Set some limits on when clients can call you, and let them know your office hours.** Creating a better balance between work and family time will help your son feel secure. You and your son could also decide on a half-hour period every day that will become your special time—time that is reserved for a favorite or unique activity or game.

○ **Create a snack drawer, where your son can help himself to healthy snacks when you are too busy to get them for him.** Once the drawer is empty, though, there will be no more snacks for the day. Choosing when to eat them is up to your son. Also, when you say no more snacks, mean no more snacks, and your son will learn to make the ones in the drawer last.

○ **Use a kitchen timer to help your son learn to be patient.** When you need to make a call, set the timer for the amount of time you believe you will be on the phone. Your son can even hold the timer if he wants, and when it beeps, he can remind you to end your call and spend some time with him.

Will these ideas keep your son from whining and begging for your attention? Well, perhaps for a while. These ideas deal with the beliefs and feelings behind your son's behavior and will help him learn to cooperate with you, but you will need to have many such conversations in the years ahead. Looking for the beliefs behind your son's behavior will help you be a calmer, more effective parent.

Learning to Listen

Most parents are really good at talking. In fact, most parents do lots and lots of talking and wonder why no one seems to be listening. The old Charlie Brown cartoons delighted generations of children (and adults) when they showed the characters going about their business while the parents and teachers went, "Waaah, waaah, waaah" somewhere off-screen. Is that really how parents sound to children? Unfortunately, sometimes it is.

Listening to your son—really listening—is one of the most encouraging things you can do for him, and one of the best ways to build a sense of belonging and connection. Listening with your full attention (not just hearing him while you make dinner or drive the car) tells him that he matters to you and that you want to know what he is thinking, feeling, and deciding to do.

Think about someone you enjoy talking to. What does that person do that allows you to feel understood and cared about? Chances are he looks at you, offers you encouraging feedback, and doesn't glance at his watch every thirty seconds.

Many of the messages we send to those we love are nonverbal—that is, they are sent without words, in our facial expressions, tones of voice, gestures, pauses, and body postures. Young children are especially sensitive to these messages and almost always can sense what you are really feeling.

Many messages your son sends you have no words; they are expressed in his actions and gestures. Be sure to make eye contact when you speak to your son and watch him when he speaks to you. Actions truly do speak louder than words when you're raising a boy; be sure you tune in to your son's nonverbal messages.

Throughout your son's growing-up years, your ability to really listen to him will be one of your most valuable parenting skills. Here are some suggestions:

○ **Make time in your day to listen.** It's fine to have conversations in the car or in the grocery store, but real listening takes time and focus. Being too busy to listen may keep you from ever really understanding your boy.

○ **Listen patiently.** Many parents take the first opportunity to jump in with suggestions, solutions, or lectures, and then wonder why their sons say, "You never listen to me!" You will know best how to help your son if you listen calmly to what he has to say. You might even ask, "Is there anything more you want to tell me?" before responding.

○ **Be sure you make eye contact.** If your son is physically smaller than you are, sit down next to him or find a way to get on the same level. (It's difficult to have a comfortable conversation with someone who towers over you!) Pay attention to your own nonverbal messages: Are you smiling? Glaring? Tapping your foot because you're anxious to be somewhere else?

○ **Be curious.** You may not share all of your son's interests or even approve of them. But the first step to solving problems is understanding, and understanding begins with listening. Invite your son to share his ideas, his joys, and his challenges with you, and take time to be genuinely curious rather than judgmental.

Listening is one of the best ways to enter your son's world and to get to know the young man he is becoming. You will always have a better idea of how to respond to your growing boy when you have taken the time to listen first.

Discovering What "Works"

There is another important key to understanding your boy as he grows and changes. For generations, parents have wondered whether environment and parenting or genes determine who a child becomes. Actually, your son's emerging personality (and much of his behavior) will be shaped by not just his inborn traits or by what he experiences but also what he decides and believes about what he experiences.

From the moment of birth, your son will watch you for clues about life. And as he observes his family and his surroundings, he will form beliefs about love and acceptance, men and women, anger, and what he must do to feel belonging and significance. These beliefs (most of which he will not be consciously aware of) will form the rules he lives his life by. Different children in the same family (despite their common genes and experiences) can make very different decisions about what "works"—and their behavior and personalities show it.

As your little boy grows, take time to consider his perceptions of your family. What is he deciding about himself, about you, and about what "works" in his world? What you discover will help you make wise parenting decisions and keep the connection between you and your son strong. Consider what makes him tick and encourages positive behavior. Does he respond positively when given a hug or some other form of physical affection? Perhaps he responds better to an earned privilege like a trip to the park.

The Message of Love

You will make many decisions during the years you are raising your son. Some of them will be easy; others will be difficult for both of you. You may believe that whatever you do, you are doing it because you love your son. But does he know that?

As the years go by, you will undoubtedly have some tough moments with your son. Setting limits, following through, and deciding what values to teach are difficult challenges for all parents, and conflict with your son is inevitable. You will learn to be kind and firm, and to follow through when necessary because you know it is best for the boy you love. But what will he think, feel, and decide about you, about himself, and about the world he lives in? It may not be what you think.

Be sure you take time every day to ask yourself if the message of love— unconditional belonging and significance—is getting through to your boy. You may not always like his behavior or his attitude. There may be moments of heartache for both of you. You and your son can survive these challenges when you share a strong connection and are willing to listen.

Conscious parenting must always be powered by love. How this love manifests itself is not always through words. Purposeful shared experiences and even showing that you value his opinion by actively listening to him express triumphs and concerns are both ways to express your love in a way that extends beyond just saying "I love you."

Important Points to Consider

Creating a sense of belonging and significance in your son's world will help him to develop healthy relationships in the years to come. Here are some points to keep in mind:

- Boys need to understand that they are loved unconditionally, despite any challenging behavior they may display.

- Active listening can help you to develop a strong relationship with your son.

- There is always a reason behind a behavior. Determining the cause will help you to find the best solutions.

CHAPTER 4

Your Infant Son

You probably know by now that the first few years of your son's life are critically important in his cognitive, social, and emotional development; they will also set the tone for your relationship in the years ahead. Even as an infant, your child is communicating with you and providing you with your first chances to listen and get to know him. Pay attention to the clues your son is giving you, be open to his emerging personality, and work at forming the bonds of trust and love that will sustain him for years to come.

Adjusting to Your Newest Family Member

Human infants are among the most helpless creatures alive. When they are born, babies cannot pick up their own heads, turn over, or move on their own. In fact, it takes a surprising amount of time for a baby to learn that those fluttery things in front of his face are his own hands and that those hands can be used to grasp and hold objects. In the beginning, your baby will sleep most of every day. (Nights may be another matter, unfortunately!)

LIFE WITH BABY

Can you remember the first time you saw your son's face? No matter how red and wrinkled he appeared, you undoubtedly fell in love at first sight. You may have dreamed of these early days and weeks together. Sometimes, though, the dreams fade a bit in the presence of reality. Your baby may cry endlessly, sleep when you're awake, wake up when you're longing for sleep, and dirty his diaper or burp up his breakfast at the most inopportune moments. You may find yourself sifting through the piles of baby gifts, wondering what a receiving blanket is for and which end of the onesie to put on first.

A good pediatrician is a must in these early months; be sure you feel comfortable asking your doctor questions, because you will have lots of them. It can also be helpful to have family and friends who have raised children before and who can be your consultants.

> In terms of physical development, babies grow from the inside out and from the top down. The first parts to be fully developed are your son's heart and lungs; the last skill he acquires is fine motor control. He will be able to pick up and move his head before coordinating his arms and legs.

No one is born knowing how to be a parent; learn all you can and don't hesitate to ask for help. As a general rule, the first few months of life with your baby boy are not a good time to worry about keeping your house spotless, entertaining your gourmet club, or landscaping your yard. Keep your life as simple as possible. Your baby will need a great deal of your time and attention, and you should make sleep and caring for yourself a priority.

PARENTING IN THE FIRST MONTHS OF LIFE

Infants are not little adults. They are astonishingly resilient and are born wired to grow and learn, but they are not able to reason, remember, or practice self-control the way you can. Never leave your baby unattended, unless he is in his crib, infant seat, or another secure place—and then only for a few moments. Many parents have had the unsettling experience of leaving a baby on a sofa or bed for "just a minute" and returning to discover that their baby chose just that moment to turn over for the first time—right onto the floor.

Many new moms experience the common mood swings known as the *baby blues*. But approximately one in ten mothers develops postpartum depression, which can interfere with her ability to bond with her baby. If you feel angry, exhausted, irritable, or ashamed; don't want to be around friends or family; or believe that you may harm your baby, ask for help right away.

Even the happiest baby will do a fair amount of crying. This is no surprise—crying is a baby's only form of communication. He will cry when he is tired, lonely, hungry, thirsty, too hot, or too cold. Sometimes he will cry just to soothe himself when he's overwhelmed with stimulation. With time and practice, you will learn to decipher your son's cries and be able to give him just what he needs.

It may seem in these first few months that everything in your life revolves around your baby, and in fact, it's probably true. By the time an infant is three months old or so, however, he usually will have settled and will have a more predictable routine. There are many resources available to help you decide about feeding, sleep habits, and physical care. No matter how overwhelmed you may occasionally feel, don't forget to take time to enjoy your son. These early months will be gone before you know it.

Brain Development

Not too long ago, even the experts believed that when a baby was born, his brain was more or less complete, and parents could focus on supplying skills and information. You may be surprised to learn, however, that your baby's brain will continue to grow within his skull for quite some time to come. In fact, the prefrontal cortex of his brain, which is located just behind his forehead, will not fully mature until he is between twenty and twenty-five years old.

HOW THE BRAIN GROWS

The human brain begins life as a small cluster of cells in the fetus. Around the fourth month of pregnancy, these cells begin to sort themselves out according to the functions they will one day perform; they then begin to migrate to the part of the brain they are designed to occupy. Some of the cells do not survive the migration; others join together in networks of connections called synapses.

Your son's brain continues to grow at an astonishing pace after he is born. By the time he is two, his brain will have the same number of synapses as yours. By the time he is three, he will have more than one thousand trillion connections—twice as many as his parents. Relationships and experience shape the wiring of the brain, so your son will depend on you for the connection and care that help him develop. Sensory stimulation, loving touch, and new experiences will help kindle your son's curiosity and development.

In fact, Alison Gopnik, PhD, Andrew N. Meltzoff, PhD, and Patricia K. Kuhl, PhD, write in *The Scientist in the Crib: What Early Learning Tells Us About the Mind* that infants have an inborn need to learn and are capable from birth of perceiving differences in faces and emotions. Babies also appear to form theories and test them by experimenting on the people and objects around them—just like adult scientists do. Researchers used to believe that an infant's brain was a blank slate, but nothing could be further from the truth!

Researchers have confirmed the existence of mirror neurons — cells in the human brain that respond both when you do an action yourself and when you watch someone else do a similar action — in humans. When you play peekaboo with your baby boy or wave bye-bye, his mirror neurons respond to your movements and prime his brain to duplicate them, beginning the lifelong process of communication, learning, and empathy.

Researchers now believe that early experiences—such as hugs from a favorite grandparent, splashing in a cold pool, or playing with finger foods—actually stimulate the growth of synapses. The brain is amazingly resilient and flexible and can adjust surprisingly well to change or injury early in life. Still, there appear to be windows during a child's growth when important skills such as language are acquired. Brain development is a use-it-or-lose-it proposition for some functions, and what is used depends largely on you.

ENCOURAGE YOUR SON'S BRAIN DEVELOPMENT

Parents across cultures and through the ages have instinctively understood how to nurture and support the healthy growth of their babies. As it turns out, much of what parents do naturally with babies seems especially designed to stimulate healthy brain growth. The nonprofit organization Parents' Action for Children offers the following suggestions for ways to connect with your baby that will also support healthy brain development:

- **Respond to your baby's cues.** Responding appropriately to the signals your baby sends is called contingent communication and is vital to his development.

○ **Touch, speak, and sing.** Holding, cuddling, talking, and singing songs communicate love and prepare your baby to learn language and social skills.

○ **Provide opportunities to play.** Play is your child's work and how he will learn about his body, movement, and the world around him. You don't need fancy baby toys; a game of pat-a-cake or crawling together on the floor will do just fine.

○ **Encourage curiosity and safe exploration.** Your son will need room to move in order to learn about his body (and gravity). Childproof your home, and then let him explore while you watch and encourage.

○ **Allow private time for your baby.** Too much stimulation can make even the calmest baby cranky. Be sure your son has time to sit and watch, to explore his own body, and to calm himself down. With experience, you will find the right balance between interaction and allowing him time to himself.

○ **Use discipline to teach—never shake or hit.** Fear and pain do not promote love and healthy learning, especially in the early years. Be sure never to use physical force to discipline your baby.

○ **Take care of yourself.** Your son can read your emotions and state of mind better than you guess. Stress, exhaustion, or depression will affect your relationship. Maternal depression can affect a baby's brain development, especially after the first six months. Caring for yourself should always be a top priority in parenting your son.

○ **Select childcare carefully.** Quality childcare can actually benefit children, but it is vitally important that you choose your son's caregivers wisely. Parents and caregivers should work together to promote healthy development in young children.

○ **Love and enjoy your child.** Remember, your son needs to know that he belongs and has worth and significance. No matter how busy you may be, never forget to tickle, laugh, and hug. Love is the most important connection of all.

Emotional Literacy

It may come as a surprise to many parents, but boys have just as many emotions (and feel them just as intensely) as girls do. In fact, as you have learned, boys may actually be more emotionally vulnerable and sensitive early in life than girls are. Emotion (rather than logic and reason) is the energy that drives the human brain. Your son's first year is an excellent time to begin building what Dan Kindlon, PhD, and Michael Thompson, PhD, call *emotional literacy*, your boy's ability to understand and express emotions clearly.

You may have taken great care to decorate your son's room and provide stimulating toys and things to look at. Your son's favorite object, however, is your face; infants prefer looking at human faces to any other thing. Gazing at your son and allowing him "face time" with you prepares him to interpret both your emotions and his own. Smile at him and watch him smile back; coo and sing and he is likely to respond with pleasure.

Many studies have found that parents spend more time talking to baby girls than they do boys; most parents tend to choose physical play with their infant sons, bouncing them, tickling them, or moving their arms and legs. Other studies have shown that boys who receive less affection tend to have greater problems with behavior in preschool. Be sure you take lots of time to talk and cuddle face to face with your boy.

Cognitive Development

You may have encountered parents whose goal is to make their child a genius from day one by surrounding him with academic stimulation. All parents want their children to succeed in life. But do babies really need flashcards and formal teaching?

Actually, no. Babies do not need formal education. The most important early learning happens in the context of relationships; your baby boy needs a connection with you. As it happens, reading together and exploring the world around you are wonderful ways to encourage an aptitude for language and learning.

Susan Gilbert reports in *A Field Guide to Boys and Girls* that the number of words spoken to an infant each day is the single most important predictor of the child's intelligence, academic success, and social abilities in the years ahead. Talking appears to stimulate the formation of connections in a child's growing brain.

Believe it or not, television (even "educational" television) does not encourage the development of language skills. Your son will learn language through conversation with you, by listening to your speech, and by beginning to imitate you. You can sing nursery rhymes (which teach the rhythms of language) together; you can sit with your son in your lap and look at board books. Point to the objects in the book and name them. Everyday life can become a wonderful laboratory for learning as you share words and ideas together. But there is no need to force or push this early learning; in fact, some experts believe that forcing children to learn before they're ready may actually make it more difficult for them to learn later on and may lead to boredom or burnout when they reach the classroom.

Perhaps the best way to encourage learning in your small son is to love learning yourself and to share with your boy the things that fascinate you. You can listen to music together, enjoy books and pictures, and chat about the world around you. You can play, and talk while you're playing. No, he won't follow every word, but he will learn from the sound of your voice and the expressions on your face. The best teaching in this first year is your loving and connected relationship with your son.

Your Son's Unique Temperament

Each child born is a unique and special person. Not surprisingly, each parent is unique, too. One of the most important tasks you face in raising your boy is learning to understand his special qualities, his strengths, and, yes, his weaknesses. He has both, and so do you. As you live and grow together, you will become more aware of the unique traits that make your son who he is. Here are some traits that may help you to understand where your son is coming from.

- **Activity.** Some children are quiet by nature, while others never stop moving. And not all active children are hyperactive. Knowing your son's activity level will help you plan his day and allow for his need for movement (or quiet).

- **Intensity.** Your son may be reserved by nature, or he may express himself in dramatic extremes. If your son is intense by nature, your job will be to help him calm down and use words to express his needs and feelings. If he is less intense, you may need to focus on drawing him out.

- **Sensitivity.** Your son may never notice that he is walking barefoot across hot gravel. Or he may flinch at the elastic in his clothing and insist that his socks are too tight. Sensitivity measures your boy's ability to handle visual, auditory, and physical stimulation. He may love a crowd or crave quiet time, and he may need your help occasionally in getting what he needs. If your son seems unusually sensitive (or lacks normal sensitivity), ask your pediatrician if an evaluation might be helpful.

- **Regularity.** Regularity refers to a child's bodily functions and need for sleep, food, and bathroom time. For example, eighteen-month-old Timmy eats all his meals on schedule and has a bowel movement at the same time every morning; his cousin Peter never follows the same routine twice.

O **Persistence.** This dimension measures a child's willingness to stay focused on a task despite frustration or lack of immediate success. Understanding your son's tolerance for frustration will give you insight about how best to teach and support him.

O **Distractibility.** Your son may be able to tune out the television, radio, and your conversations with friends to focus on his game or book, or every noise and movement in the room may distract him. Distractibility is often a factor in how well a child performs in school.

O **Approach or withdrawal.** Some babies accept new people, foods, and toys eagerly, while others turn their heads away or refuse to try something new. If your son is slow to approach, you can help him best by showing patience and acceptance and by teaching coping skills as he grows.

O **Adaptability.** You may be blessed with a baby who will go anywhere, sleep anywhere, nurse anywhere, and be happy anywhere. Or you may have an infant who desperately needs familiar surroundings and people to feel secure. Children low in adaptability will need extra help from parents as they experience change in their daily routines.

O **Mood.** Some children (like some adults) see the glass as half empty, while others see it as half full. Mood—the tendency toward optimism or negativity—appears to be an inborn trait. Rather than blaming or trying to fix your little one, you can work on ways to help him see the positive side of life.

Remember, temperament traits are no one's fault—especially not your son's. They appear to be part of the package human beings are born with, and wise parents will learn to shape, encourage, and teach rather than blame, lecture, or nag. Knowing your son's comfort level and preferences will give you clues about how to make each day as enjoyable and easy as possible. Knowing your own temperament will help you plan for those times when your temperament and his don't mesh well and accept them as part of the process of raising your son.

The Importance of Touch for Boys

Boys need tender touch. And for many parents, particularly fathers, offering loving touch to boys may feel wrong. If you hold your son too often, will it make him weak? Will you spoil him? If you offer him hugs and cuddles, will he be less masculine as he grows up?

Babies who are massaged, touched, and held often are less irritable and gain weight more quickly than babies who are not touched. Touch is a powerful means of communication, especially with an infant who does not yet understand words.

THE POWER OF TOUCH

Touch is one of the first messages your son receives from you: If you are happy to see him and pleased with his behavior, you are likely to touch him gently, lovingly, and perhaps for longer. If he has cried all afternoon and refused to take a nap, and now you have to change his diaper, your touch may be rougher, brisker, and less affectionate. Either way, your little boy is learning about you, about himself, and about what works in his new family.

CHALLENGES OF TOUCH FOR FATHERS

Touch can be difficult for many fathers, who may not have experienced loving touch from their own parents or who may believe the subtle message of our culture that boys should somehow need less physical affection and contact than girls. Yet study after study has shown that fathers are crucial to their sons' emotional and intellectual development. If you are the father of a baby boy, you can help him best by being directly involved in his care. Take time to change diapers and to comfort him when he cries. Smile at him, hold him, and rock him. Wrestling and roughhousing are great, but be sure there is time for tender touch as well.

As your son grows, touch may be more effective than words in communicating love and encouragement. Ruffling your son's hair, rubbing his back, and offering him a hug when life is overwhelming are all ways of building connection and sending the message of love.

Should You Discipline a Baby?

Active, healthy babies do many things that worry, annoy, or irritate their parents. Your son is busy learning all about the world around him, and everything is an exciting experiment. Dropping toys and food is a great way to learn about gravity; ripping paper makes noise and feels good. Your son does not yet feel completely comfortable in his own body, so each day may be a little different from the one before it. He may decide that shrieking is entertaining and do it for hours. He may love to climb the furniture. And for some reason, little boys are quick to discover remote controls and telephones. Sometimes parents worry that, without discipline, their small son will become a terror.

Your baby does not yet have the ability to connect cause and effect, so tools such as time-out and consequences will not work until he is older. The best discipline for your baby boy is lots of supervision, physically removing him from things he should not touch, and redirecting him toward acceptable activities.

You may be pleased to know that you can relax about discipline, especially during the first year of your son's life. He does not need discipline in the traditional sense; in fact, when most parents talk about *discipline*, they really mean *punishment*. And babies do not need punishment at all.

The literal meaning of the word *discipline* is *to teach*. In fact, the word comes from the same Latin root as the word *disciple*. What your son needs during his first year—and in fact, throughout your years together—is lots and lots of teaching. And teaching happens best where there is patience, kindness, and respect.

Parents often believe that a boy requires more discipline than a girl, and sometimes are quick to use physical means to "teach him a lesson." However, your son will learn to respect limits (and you) as he acquires language and emotional skills, and as he builds a loving and respectful relationship with you. Most of the time, a firm voice and the willingness to get up and gently move your baby away from forbidden objects are the best approaches—and, yes, you will have to do them many times. Words alone are never effective discipline with a young child, and yelling will only make both of you feel terrible. Kind, firm action and lots of teaching are best.

Important Points to Consider

The first year of your son's life will be a time of tremendous growth and development. Here are some points to consider:

O Parenting is not a skill you are born with. It's okay to ask questions!

O Responding to your baby's cues, like crying or cooing, will help you to build a connection.

O Infant boys need just as much touch and emotional support as infant girls do.

 **CHAPTER 5**

The Preschool Years

If you've spent any time at all around preschool boys, you probably won't be surprised to learn that human beings never have more physical energy than they do at the age of three. There is no question that little boys can be a handful; they are energetic, impulsive, and funny. They are curious and occasionally defiant. But they are also charming, affectionate, and compassionate. The preschool years are busy, often challenging ones, but they are precious, too. Welcome to the world of the preschool boy!

Creating a Safe Environment

While it's never wise to generalize about human beings, there are definitely a few things parents can learn from the differences between boys and girls during the preschool years, roughly the ages of eighteen months to six years old. Most of the available research tells us that as a group, little boys tend to be more physically active, competitive, and, yes, aggressive than little girls. If you always expect your toddler son to sit quietly in a restaurant or in church and follow the rules, you will be disappointed at least some of the time.

Boys like to move. Before their first birthdays, they experience a surge of physical energy that will last for quite some time. Each boy is an individual, and one of the most important tasks you face as a parent is learning to know and understand your unique son. Still, most boys do love to run, climb, wrestle, dig, and explore. If there's a locked drawer or a dark closet, sooner or later your son is likely to discover it, and he will want to unearth its secrets.

A VOYAGE OF SELF-DISCOVERY

You will need to remind yourself often during these busy years that your little boy truly does not plan to defy or frustrate you. Young children do not acquire the ability to tie cause and effect together, make formal plans, or think things through reasonably until they are around three years old. It may appear that your son deliberately sets out each day to do all the things you have specifically forbidden, but that really is not what is happening.

Life in your son's world is an ongoing experiment, a marvelous laboratory where he can learn about himself, others, and the world he inhabits. Little boys learn by doing, by touching and holding and throwing. Your son is busy learning about himself; your job as his parent is to supervise, protect, set reasonable limits when necessary, and follow through with kindness, firmness, and respect.

CHILDPROOFING

Some parents believe that a house should never be childproofed. Instead, they claim, the child should be *house-proofed*, taught never to touch fragile items or enter off-limits rooms. Boys certainly need to learn to respect limits and look without touching. But learning these skills is a process that takes time and patience. In the meantime, wise parents learn to create some safe space for their active little boys. Consider the following suggestions.

Boys' occasional impulsiveness may lead to daredevil and defiant behavior when they're young. Without teaching and guidance, it can lead to problems with drug and alcohol abuse, promiscuity, and defiance against authority later on. These early years are the time to build a respectful relationship with your son and to practice setting reasonable limits.

Safety Comes First

Be sure that as soon as your son becomes mobile you cover electrical outlets, put latches on drawers and cupboards, and put chemicals and cleaning supplies well out of reach. Check electrical appliances to be sure they can't be turned on and that cords are not frayed or easily chewed on. It is also wise to use safety gates around stairways and to be sure that pools are fenced. Accidents are a constant danger to curious little ones; be sure you take the time to prevent as many as you can.

Put Breakables Out of Reach

Keep breakable items away from your son, at least for now. Your three-year-old may know that he shouldn't touch your china figurines, but he just can't resist holding one. Your son's sense of belonging and safety is more valuable than even the most precious collection. Put the fragile items away until he has better impulse control. It will save you many painful (and unnecessary) arguments.

Create Safe Spaces

Make sure you have created childproof areas of your home where your son is welcome to play and explore. You may want to leave the pantry or a cupboard unlatched so your son can stack cans or play with the plastic containers. If you can handle the noise, pots and pans make great drum sets, and most little boys love to bang away from time to time. Or you can set up a play space in a corner of a family area where you can be sure your son is protected and where there are items he will enjoy.

Make Time for Active Play

It can be helpful to build time into every day for your son to run, climb, and be physically active in acceptable, safe ways. Quiet times will work better for both of you when he's also had time to zoom.

Language and Social Skills

Believe it or not, children have to learn how to play. Your son's earliest playmates will undoubtedly be you and the children he encounters at preschool, your friends' homes, and the park. In these early encounters, play is more likely to be conducted side by side than face to face.

Very young children engage in what is called parallel play—that is, they tend to sit together, each playing independently. They are in the same space, and they are playing, but they are not playing together. Eventually, a child will begin to notice other children and express curiosity about these strange beings. A little boy is likely to explore his new acquaintance by touching or poking him or by grabbing at a toy to see what he will do.

LANGUAGE AND PLAY

Not surprisingly, social relationships tend to work out better when a child has learned to use his words. It also helps when a child has acquired some emotional skills and can read faces and body language to understand whether or not to approach a new person. It has been noted in several studies that girls tend to be more collaborative in their play; they talk and make rules together about how their game will go. Boys often form groups with a leader, and the chosen activity is usually physical.

Your son will need time and opportunities to practice his social skills. Be sure you offer him opportunities to be with children his own age. When things go awry (and they inevitably will), don't punish or scold; instead, take time to explore with your son what happened, why it happened, and what he could do to get a better result next time.

One psychologist found that mothers of daughters talk more with their children about sadness and ways to solve problems; mothers of sons talk about anger and ways to get even. Use curiosity questions such as "What was your favorite part of the day?" and "What do you think could have made your day better?" along with gentle coaching with your son to help him understand feelings and resolve conflicts with his friends.

HITTING AND AGGRESSION

Boys are certainly more prone to physical aggression and competition than are girls. They may kick, bite, or throw things when they feel frustrated or defeated. Speech experts believe that some aggressive activity may be related to the development of language; children who are slower to speak clearly often experience frustration and express it in the form of anger or defiance.

Your son needs to learn that hurting himself, another person, or property is never acceptable. But hurting *him* will not teach that lesson. Instead, always take a moment to calm down first and consider the root cause of the behavior, and then help him do the same. Remove your son gently from the situation or other children if necessary. Then, when both you and he are able to talk calmly, look together for solutions to the problem.

If other children are involved, it is helpful to explore what they might have been feeling. You can also tell your son how you are feeling; for example, "I feel sad and worried when you kick the dog" or "It hurts when you hit me, and I cannot allow you to do that." Stay calm; raising your own voice never helps.

THE ART OF SHARING

Sharing is difficult. In fact, you may know several adults who can't do it very well. For young children (who haven't yet accepted that they are not the center of the family universe), it's often downright impossible. Sharing becomes important to parents and teachers as children reach the age of three or four and are more likely to have younger siblings or to be part of groups of children. "Share with your little sister," you might say to your son. Unfortunately, until he's had some training and practice, he is likely to respond by jutting out his lip and pulling harder on his toy.

You can help your son learn to share by taking time to teach. Remember, your son does not know how to negotiate or compromise and may not have a fully functional vocabulary (or a great deal of self-control). You can model sharing by showing him what it looks like: "Here's a cookie. I'll have a piece, and I'll share a piece with you." Or you can show him how to take turns: "I'll throw the ball to you, and then you throw it to me."

You can also coach children to use words together. For example, you might say, "I can see that you want Jessie's toy. What could you say to her?" If your son says, "May I please have the toy?" you can smile, and then help Jessie figure out how to respond. (Please note that the answer does not always have to be "yes." "Maybe later" is an appropriate answer, too.)

Like most of the skills and concepts adults take for granted, sharing is an art that must be practiced over and over again. As in so many other areas of life with your son, you can be his best teacher and example.

Brain researchers tell us that autobiographical memory does not develop until a child is approximately two years old. Until then, your son's sense of self and sense of time are not like yours; he is probably telling you the truth when he tells you that he "can't remember" something that happened.

It will take lots of practice for your son to learn to get along easily with his peers, and even the best of friends sometimes disagree. Keep your cool, keep everyone safe, and be prepared to do lots of patient teaching as your son learns about friendship.

Nurture Empathy

Many studies have shown that young children are very sensitive to the feelings of others, and boys may be even more perceptive than girls. Empathy appears to be an inborn trait for most preschoolers, but it can be lost over time without thoughtful nurturing. Here are some suggestions for nurturing empathy in your growing son:

O Build a secure attachment with your boy. A strong connection with caring adults is essential for the growth of empathy.

O Use lots of feeling words like "sad," "scared," and "excited" with your little boy. In order to empathize with others, children must recognize their own feelings and believe those feelings are accepted and understood.

O Discipline should help a child feel safe and calm, rather than agitated or rejected. Physical punishment and withdrawing affection make it difficult for young boys to feel empathy toward others.

O Talk often about the feelings and experiences of others, especially when watching television or news footage of natural disasters or conflict. Help your son explore what others might be thinking and feeling.

O Model empathy and compassion yourself. Your actions will always be your son's best example.

Try to Understand Your Son's World

Even the most loving parent sometimes assumes that a young child thinks, feels, and experiences life as adults do. Nothing could be further from the truth. Sometime soon, try the following experiment: Get down on your knees. (Yes, really.) Now crawl from your son's bedroom to the kitchen. How long does it take you to get there? What do you see along the way? Is it easy to reach the things you need? If there is an adult handy, look up at her. Wow, she's pretty big, isn't she? What does she look like if she's angry?

Now imagine going for a walk to the park. Imagine holding the adult's hand and notice how soon you want to pull your own hand away—not because you're feeling defiant but because the blood stops flowing when you hold your arm up too long. Adults walk quickly, don't they? It's hard to keep up, especially when you want to stop and look at the flowers, the cool bug you find in the dirt, or the neighbor's new puppy.

Spending a few moments in your little boy's shoes can be an immensely helpful experience. Despite what you may have believed, the world of a young child is very different from the world of an adult. Finding ways to understand your son's world may be one of the most valuable conscious parenting skills you will ever learn.

Encouraging Curiosity

It isn't easy being a parent. You undoubtedly feel fatigued and stressed at least some of the time; raising your son is almost certainly not the only thing on your daily agenda. Sometimes all you really want is for your son to just listen and obey without a whimper. Unfortunately, during the preschool years, even the most cooperative little boy will struggle to comply with adult expectations. There's just too much else going on in his world.

You will be far more successful at setting limits, communicating, and getting along with your small son when you take time to be curious about who he is becoming and what his world is like. Here are some things to ponder:

O Preschoolers do not experience time in the same way adults do. Five minutes for you may feel like an hour for your son. If you expect patience, you will both be disappointed in the results.

O Preschoolers are far more interested in the process than the product. You may want a painting to hang on your refrigerator; your son may have found smearing the paint with his fingers satisfying enough, and he may have no interest in doing more.

- Preschoolers cannot tell fantasy from reality the way you can. If it happens on the movie screen or on television, it's "real" and no amount of debate can convince him otherwise. (This fact is a good reason to exercise caution when the media is concerned.)

- Preschoolers love to ask questions. While the constant stream of "whys" and "how comes" can be exhausting, questions are truly how little boys learn. Be sure to take time to listen to your son, too.

Curiosity about your son's perceptions, his feelings, and his ideas is always a good place to begin as you solve problems and face challenges together. Curiosity will carry you from the early years through adolescence to the day your son leaves to begin his own independent life. Take time to express curiosity before passing judgment; it will always help you parent your son wisely.

Mealtime Challenges

Young children and their parents often disagree about eating. Parents tend to like the idea of three meals a day; they want their children to eat healthy food, eat what is put in front of them without complaining, and cooperate about snacks and other food choices. Eating is actually much simpler than most parents make it: You should eat when you are hungry and stop when you are full. When parents force children to eat, punish them for avoiding certain foods, provide sugary snacks, or cook meals on demand, they usually interfere with the natural process of eating.

You may worry about your son's eating because you want him to be healthy. It may help you relax to know that children usually eat what they need over time (barring illness or other special circumstances). In other words, your son may not eat all of the food groups every day. In fact, he may want to live on macaroni and cheese for days at a time. But if your son is active and healthy, he will usually choose to eat what he needs—eventually.

SUPPLY HEALTHY FOOD

Your job is to make good food available; your son's job is to eat it. A little junk food won't damage your son permanently (you don't need to take away his Halloween candy, for instance), but do limit the amount of fatty, sugary treats available on a regular basis. Instead, provide fruits, vegetables, dairy, and other healthy snacks.

MAKE FAMILY MEALS A TRADITION

Try to get your family together for supper each night, but don't force your son to eat. Studies have shown that when a family sits down to eat a meal together at least three times a week, children do better at school, choose better behavior, and are less likely to abuse drugs or alcohol. Be sure, however, that family meals are a pleasure rather than a battle. It is helpful to provide at least one item that you know your son will eat happily. Invite him to try new things, but don't leave him sitting at the table alone, staring at his unwanted lima beans. He will learn only to resist both you and eating. An important part of conscious parenting, at the table and elsewhere, is focusing on connection and conversation.

GET CHILDREN INVOLVED

Get your son involved in meal planning, shopping, and food preparation. Children love to be invited; they usually resist being commanded. When your son is old enough, invite him to help you plan meals. You can give him his own short grocery list (use pictures if he cannot read yet) and help him shop. Even toddlers can rinse lettuce, put cheese slices on hamburger buns, and bring napkins to the table. Your son is more likely to eat something he has helped prepare.

COOKING TO ORDER

Beware the habit of cooking meals to order! One frazzled mother of three young boys found herself cooking three meals every night. "They won't eat if I don't give them what they want," she said. Providing special service for your son will only create a demand for more of the same. Prepare one meal for the family; if your son refuses to eat it, let him know when the next meal will be. If your son is old enough, you might give him the choice of making himself a sandwich or another simple food. Remember to be kind and firm at the same time.

All children go through phases with their eating, and some actually do better when they are allowed to graze rather than having to wait for the next scheduled meal. Relax and do your best to create peaceful, nourishing mealtimes—and give your son a good multivitamin.

CREATING A HEALTHY LIFESTYLE

If you have been watching the news recently, you are undoubtedly aware that doctors are increasingly concerned about childhood obesity. Weight gain that happens early in life tends to set patterns that are difficult to change later and may lead to lifelong health problems such as diabetes and hypertension. The preschool years are the perfect time to help your son learn to live a healthy life.

It is generally unwise to put your young son on a diet. Pediatricians agree that limiting food intake for growing children tends to set up power struggles and create emotional issues that are often as damaging as the physical ones. It is wiser to focus on the long-term: Pay attention to nutrition, encourage exercise, and take your son to his doctor for regular checkups.

Of course, you will always be your son's best teacher. If you sit in front of the television all day snacking on chips and cookies, you will have a hard time convincing him that he shouldn't do the same. If you get regular exercise, eat reasonably healthy food, and limit television, video games, and other passive activities, your son will be more likely to learn good habits.

The best way to help your boy have an appetite for healthy food is to encourage healthy activity. This can be difficult for working parents whose children are in childcare programs, but do your best to keep your son active. Plan fun family activities and enjoy working up a good appetite together.

Foster Healthy Sleep Habits

Sleep, whether at night or during naptime, is another thing you cannot make a child do, but that doesn't stop parents from trying. Young children learn best through repetition and consistency. Create a routine for any part of your day that is challenging, such as mealtimes, bedtime, or getting out the door in the morning. Make a routine picture chart with your son, not for rewards but to map the order of the activity. Knowing what comes next will help your son cooperate.

You will help your son develop healthy sleep patterns when you learn what helps him relax, and all children are different. Some like a night-light; others want it dark. Some want background noise so they don't feel alone; others need complete silence. Some want to be warm, while others prefer to be cool. There is no right way to sleep; what matters is that your son is comfortable, secure, and relaxed.

Instead of trying to make your son go to sleep, focus on helping him feel sleepy. A game or a walk outdoors before bed may help him feel tired; a warm bath may help him relax. Include stories, songs, and hugs in your bedtime routine. Then, when your son is in bed, give him a kiss and leave him to fall asleep. If he gets up, kindly and firmly return him to his bed. Your son will know when you are serious and when he cannot manipulate you by whining or crying.

Having a snuggle in bed together when your son is sick or has a nightmare is fine, but eventually he will need to learn to sleep on his own. Let him know you want him to sleep in his own room; do his bedtime routine there and carry him back if he creeps into your bed. It may take time, but be kind, firm, and consistent.

Your son needs his sleep, but when you're an active little boy, it is hard to slow down long enough to rest. Kindness, firmness, and effective routines will help you create healthy sleep habits.

Managing Potty Training

Like it or not, most boys are slower to use the toilet than girls are. In fact, the average age for day and nighttime dryness is around three and a half years old. That may not be good news to moms and dads who are anxious for the diaper days to end. Still, toilet training depends on both physical awareness and self-control, and your son will need to master these abilities before he is successful in the bathroom.

Children have an uncanny ability to sense the issues that are important to parents. If you worry about eating, they will resist food. If you insist on bedtime, they aren't sleepy. And if you make toilet training a battle, they will fight you. Unfortunately, toileting battles can have serious health implications. Forcing your son to use the toilet before he's ready may cause him to withhold his stool, and that can cause severe constipation and an impacted bowel.

To successfully master the bathroom, your son needs to be able to read the physical signals that tell him he has to go. He needs to be willing to leave his play and be able to undo his buttons or snaps. You can help by letting him see what happens in the bathroom, like you brushing your teeth or washing your hands, without expecting him to join in. You can provide a diet rich in fiber. And you can understand that your son, too, experiences stress (like following the birth of a younger sibling) and that stress may affect his bowel and urination habits.

As with so many other challenges, you must set the stage and encourage your son to do his part. When accidents happen, do your best to remain calm. If appropriate, teach your son to clean himself up without lectures or blame. If you have serious concerns, take time to check with your son's pediatrician.

Use Technology Sparingly

In recent years, toy store shelves and magazine pages have become increasingly crowded with educational products for preschoolers. Many parents wonder if their sons need all these sophisticated games and gizmos in order to be successful in school and in life.

While these products may be fun for children (and parents) to play with, they are not necessary. It's worth repeating that all important early learning happens in the context of relationships; what your son needs is lots of time and teaching from you. He will learn social, language, and life skills by spending time with you—not from a computer, no matter how well designed. You can add technological toys to your lives if you so desire, but they are not required to grow a happy, healthy, successful son. He will have lots of time to learn about computers and technology as he enters school.

Conscious living requires the ability to reflect and spend time as a family. Although technology certainly has benefits, it can be an all-consuming distraction. Finding a balance between the use of technology and other quiet learning activities is difficult, but as a parent, you are there to help navigate this technologically focused world.

Important Points to Consider

The preschool years are an active and exciting time for most children. Here are several points to keep in mind when interacting with your preschool-aged son:

O Creating an environment that is physically safe for your preschool-aged son is a must.

O Your son will need time to develop social skills, be active, and simply play!

O Getting down on your son's level, both emotionally and physically, will help you to understand his behavior and responses.

O Involving your son in your daily activities will teach him new skills, improve his self-esteem, and foster a positive connection.

CHAPTER 6

The Emotional Life of Boys

Despite the fact that boys are often more emotionally sensitive early in life and develop social and emotional skills more slowly than do girls, the emotional wiring in male and female brains is essentially the same. Yet you'll find that many people around you (maybe even in your own family) still believe that while girls should be able to cry, giggle, and be afraid, boys should not. The truth is that boys have just as many emotions as girls do and must learn to express them in appropriate ways. You must be open to your son's emotions and allow him to feel and experience them rather than having him shut down or cover them up. Communication and an honest look at how you handle your own emotions will be key to helping your son.

The Danger of the Stoic Male

Many human societies throughout history have been patriarchal, meaning that men run the government, own the property, and assume responsibility for providing for women and children. Many religions bolster the notion that men are inherently more responsible and reliable, while women are relegated to a secondary position, keeping the home and raising the children. In earlier times, the very survival of a community and its families depended on a man's strength—his ability to hunt, farm, and provide shelter and security for those in his care.

Few families these days depend on Dad to hunt down dinner, but some of those early cultural beliefs about gender remain. Among the strongest are the notions we hold about men and women, boys and girls, and what they should (or should not) feel.

THE BOY CODE

In his book *Real Boys: Rescuing Our Sons from the Myths of Boyhood*, William Pollack, PhD, describes what he calls the *Boy Code*, the culturally ingrained code of acceptable behavior that dictates what boys can feel— and what they cannot. This code leads boys to say they are okay when they are not, avoid asking for help, and run from any appearance of softness or weakness.

Pollack writes, "The Boy Code is so strong, yet so subtle, in its influence that boys may not even know they are living their lives in accordance with it. In fact, they may not realize there is such a thing until they violate the code in some way or try to ignore it. When they do, however, society tends to let them know—swiftly and forcefully—in the form of a taunt by a sibling, a rebuke by a parent or a teacher, or ostracism by classmates."

Think about the last time you saw a boy get hurt at a baseball or soccer game. When a boy rises and limps off the field of combat, the spectators applaud and cheer. The message is clear: Boys should not show pain or fear. Boys must stay strong even when they're hurt.

As it turns out, boys have the same range of emotions wired into their brains as girls do. So what accounts for the different beliefs we have about boys, girls, and emotions?

Emotions and the Brain

You may remember *Star Trek*, the 1960s classic television program. One of the leading characters on that program, Mr. Spock, came from a race that felt no emotions. Spock operated on pure logic; his decisions were dictated by reason rather than messy, unreliable emotions. Many adults long for a similarly uncluttered way of life, but the truth is that emotion is vital to human existence, and managing emotions well is a significant part of being healthy and happy.

Researchers have believed for some time that emotion (rather than logic) is the driving force in the human brain. Recent studies show that emotion may actually be the link that connects the various functions of the brain and helps them work together. In other words, emotion integrates the different parts of the brain.

Emotions are the data you need to make decisions and stay safe. When you feel lonely, you need companionship. When you are afraid, you need to protect yourself. If you are aware of your emotions and learn to pay attention to them, you will always know what you need to be healthy. Being a conscious parent to your son includes helping him identify and respond to his emotions in the same way.

Some researchers tell us that emotion ties together physiological, cognitive, sensory, and social processes, allowing our bodies, thoughts, and senses to work together. Rather than being messy feelings that complicate our lives (best kept private or stuffed away altogether), emotions actually may be responsible for neural integration, keeping us sane, healthy, and functioning effectively. Emotion appears to be the linking force that allows the different parts of our brain to talk to each other.

It is all the more tragic, then, that our culture effectively discourages boys from understanding and feeling their emotions. Numerous writers and researchers, among them Michael Thompson, Dan Kindlon, Terrence Real, William Pollack, and Michael Gurian, have noted the silent crisis that occurs when boys lose the ability to connect with their feelings. Boys are at greater risk for depression, suicide, academic problems, and drug and alcohol abuse than are girls, often because they not only lack the ability to identify their emotions accurately and learn from them, but they also actively suppress their feelings. If emotion is intended by nature to keep your son healthy, how can you teach him to understand his feelings, to manage them effectively, and to behave with thoughtfulness and flexibility in a world that does not make a boy's emotional journey easy?

Building Emotional Literacy

All too often, boys learn that the ideal man is the strong, silent type. Many boys have exactly two speeds when it comes to emotion: They are *okay*, or they are *angry*. Many parents are shocked at how quickly their sons become belligerent, but it should come as no surprise. Anger is culturally acceptable for boys (and men) and creates its own set of problems.

Perhaps the most devastating emotion young boys experience as they grow up is shame. No one enjoys shame, but boys may actually fear it. Shame strikes at a boy's heart; it causes him to close down and avoid connection with adults at the very time he needs it most. Discipline for your son should never involve humiliation or shame.

In *I Don't Want to Talk about It: Overcoming the Secret Legacy of Male Depression*, psychotherapist Terrence Real talks about the emotional numbing that boys experience as they grow up. They begin life as exuberant, lively little people with a full range of feelings, but after they have spent some time in school, they have discovered what *real men* are like and they begin to restrict their expressiveness. Research shows that most males struggle not only to express but also to identify their emotions. The formal term for this difficulty is *alexithymia*, and psychologist Ron Levant, EdD, MBA, estimates that as many as 80 percent of men in our society have a mild to severe form of it. If you ask most men what they are feeling, you are likely to hear what they are *thinking* instead. Men (and their sons) often find it difficult to tell the difference. These emotional issues are not the result of differences in the brain; they are most likely differences in what boys and girls learn from parents, peers, and their culture as they grow to maturity.

TEACH EMOTIONAL VOCABULARY

Boys are healthier and happier when they have solid emotional resources and access to all of the varied and intricate parts of themselves. How can parents teach boys to have a rich emotional life and deep connections to others and still be full members in the society of men?

To build emotional literacy in your son, you should start by teaching him an emotional vocabulary. From the time your son is an infant, speak to him with a rich and varied emotional vocabulary. Babies are not born with words for their feelings; they must be taught. You can say, "You look sad" or "You must feel disappointed" without rescuing or pampering your son. You can also talk about your own feelings without making your son responsible for them. When you say, "I felt scared; did you?" to your boy, you give him permission to feel and express his own emotions.

You must be sure to model connection and empathy for your son. Mothers and fathers can demonstrate by their own actions what real love and connection look like. When your son lives surrounded with respect, love, understanding, and empathy, he will find it easier to practice those skills himself.

Be sure to actively listen to your son. Then listen some more. One of the best ways to encourage expression is simply to listen without judgment. Show empathy; don't rush to offer solutions. Repeat back what you have heard, to ensure that you heard him correctly. Remember, you don't have to agree with your son's feelings to listen, nor do you have to accept inappropriate behavior. Listening well is the first step to creating connections and solving problems together.

In addition to listening and teaching your son an emotional vocabulary, make room for your son to be himself. Avoid telling your son what he should or should not feel; give him room to explore his strengths and weaknesses in a safe environment. When your son doesn't need to fear shame or rejection, he can express his emotions, needs, and dreams openly.

Boys and Anger

Anger has long been an acceptable emotion in boys and men. After all, the reasoning goes, they have lots of testosterone; they can't help being aggressive. Indeed, physical expressions of anger, including fistfights or other confrontations, are often seen as true masculine behavior. Even in these supposedly enlightened times, a boy who walks away from a fight may be called a coward.

Numerous studies have shown that there is no real difference in the way men and women *experience* anger. All people feel anger, and most feel angry about the same things. However, men and women (and boys and girls) *express* their anger in different ways. Men tend to be more physically aggressive, engage in passive-aggressive behavior more often, and can be more impulsive in expressing anger. Women stay angry longer, are more resentful, and often use relationships as weapons in expressing anger (such as excluding a former friend, starting unpleasant rumors, or insulting someone's appearance).

Some experts believe that boys are prone to anger because it is a substitute for other, less culturally acceptable emotions, such as sadness and loneliness. Parents, too, contribute to boys' anger; research has shown that parents encourage daughters to resolve conflicts peacefully but allow boys to retaliate. Anger is a normal part of the human emotional spectrum; in fact, anger is often what motivates us to solve problems, stand up for ourselves, and attempt to right the wrongs of the world. Misdirected anger, however, can cause great harm.

MANAGING ANGER

Everyone gets angry from time to time; your son will, too. How you respond to his anger will teach him about how to recognize and manage it as he grows. First, though, you must learn to deal with your own anger effectively. If you yell, scream, and throw things, your son will, too. Admit your own strong feelings, accept them, take a time-out when necessary, and focus on solving problems rather than spreading blame.

Psychologist Daniel Goleman notes that it is considered appropriate for women to express fear and sadness, and for men to express anger. However, if a woman is in a position of power in business or government, anger becomes an appropriate emotion for her. Most of our beliefs about feelings are rooted in culture.

You must then teach your son that anger is acceptable, but hurting people or things is not. You can help your son learn that he can feel angry without hurting himself or someone else. Accept his anger and offer him ways to cool down when he needs them. Then, when everyone is calm, sit down and explore ways to make the situation better.

One option you could explore when teaching your son how to deal with anger is to create an anger wheel of choice with him. Sometime when you are both calm, make a pie chart with suggestions for things he can do when he is angry. (Be sure all of the suggestions are okay with you!) Options might include taking a time-out, listening to music, calling a friend, or shooting baskets in the backyard. Then, when your son is upset, he can look at the wheel of choice for ideas. Having solutions already at hand will help him calm down more quickly.

Finally, learn to listen to your son's real feelings and help him find words to express them. Your son's body language, facial expressions, and gestures will help you to comprehend what he is feeling. Gently help him pair his words with emotions before he reaches the boiling point. Anger is often a smoke screen for other, deep-rooted feelings such as fear or hurt; when your son develops a sense of inner awareness and communicates these feelings openly to you, displays of anger may no longer be necessary.

Boys and Depression

Far too many boys suffer from serious depression, especially during adolescence. Depressed boys may be hard to spot; they don't always sulk in their rooms, looking sad and lonely. Depression in boys often takes the form of rage, extreme irritability, or drug and alcohol use. Depressed boys may avoid school, stop doing their work, and become increasingly disconnected from parents and friends. They may even begin to talk about suicide.

Every year there is an average of 1,890 suicides among fifteen- to nineteen-year-olds; 1,625 of them are committed by boys. Girls attempt suicide more often, but boys' attempts are more lethal, often because boys have been unable to express sadness and isolation. As a conscious parent you must keep a strong connection with your son and should not hesitate to get professional help when needed.

Many experts believe that boys' susceptibility to depression stems from the lack of connection they often feel with parents and other adults. Grief and loss, such as a death or the divorce of parents, can also trigger depression.

The best way to prevent depression and other emotional problems is to stay connected, actively listen and accept, and spend time just being together. Sometimes, though, boys suffer from depression despite the best efforts of their parents. How can you tell if your son is struggling with depression? Keep an eye out for the following behaviors that could be signs of depression:

- **Frequent, angry outbursts or impulsive behavior.** All boys have a bad mood now and then, but depression often leads boys to become increasingly hostile and filled with rage.

- **Lack of interest in activities and friends he used to enjoy.** He may appear bored, exhausted, or listless and may be "too tired" to participate in sports or other activities. He may also argue with friends more often, or report that he has no friends.

- **Changes in sleep patterns, eating, or weight.** He may sleep all the time or tell you he can't sleep at all. He may report that he's not hungry when he hasn't eaten a solid meal for days.

- **Low self-esteem.** He may express harsh criticism of himself, see only his failures, and lose confidence in his ability to succeed at a task.

- **Increased risky behaviors.** A depressed boy may begin taking unnecessary chances; teenagers may drive too fast, drink too much too often, or experiment with drugs.

- **Difficulty with academic work.** He may lose interest in schoolwork, skip classes, refuse to do homework, and bring home lower grades.

It's important to note that none of these symptoms alone means your son is depressed or at risk for suicide. However, if you begin to notice several of these signals, or any other marked change in your son's mood or behavior, it is wise to pay attention and to make an extra effort to draw him out. If you are concerned about your son's emotional health, don't hesitate to find a skilled therapist who can work with your son to help him resolve these issues. Depression isn't weakness; it can be healed with time and care.

Keep Connected to Your Son

Too many boys lack the emotional awareness and resiliency they need to live happy and successful lives. You may have been more concerned about your son's grades and behavior than his emotional health, but your son depends on you to keep him connected, teach him emotional literacy, and help him identify and express his feelings. Emotions are not just for girls. All healthy human beings have them and must learn to manage them effectively.

You may worry that teaching your son emotional awareness and talking openly about feelings may make him too fragile to survive in the world. In truth, adding the language of emotion to your lives together can only make him stronger. You can honor his pride and his innate boyness at the same time that you teach him to be connected to his inner self and to those around him.

Your son may hesitate to talk openly about feelings, but he probably won't mind being asked for help in solving problems. You can learn a great deal about the way he sees the world by inviting his opinion on issues and challenges you face together. What does he think about his friends' behavior? What would make his school a better place? Is there a way to make household chores fairer for everyone? It is in the context of these everyday topics that you can connect with your boy.

Your son will need your help to develop courage and to learn to be the best boy—and eventually, the best man—he can be. Accept all the parts of your son, his strengths and weaknesses, his thoughts and emotions. Love and awareness will help you keep him whole and guide him toward a healthy, successful life.

Important Points to Consider

Despite certain myths, boys experience strong emotions—and a wide range of emotions as well, not just the accepted emotion of anger. Here are some points to keep in mind about your son and his emotions:

O The way that you respond to your emotions will have a profound impact on your son. Be mindful of how you handle yourself in front of your son.

O Boys are happier and healthier when they have strong emotional resources to draw from. Teach your son an emotional vocabulary so he can have the words he needs to express himself.

- Though there is no real difference in the anger that boys and girls feel, boys are often taught to deal with it differently.

- Boys have a high risk of depression often due to being forced to bottle up emotions. Focusing on a strong connection and open communication can help your son to cope in difficult situations.

 **CHAPTER 7**

Fathers and Sons

Fathers are different from mothers. They look different, they sound different, they often play in a different way, and they usually have a different approach to raising children than mothers do. And that's a good thing. A boy learns from his father, without even realizing he's doing it, what a man is and does. He learns about masculinity, about what men like and don't like. Many adult men report that when they were boys they either wanted to be just like their dads or wanted to be the exact opposites. Fathers undoubtedly have a powerful influence on their growing sons, and it begins from the moment of birth. Many men spend a lifetime longing for a father's love and approval. How can you as a father create a secure, loving relationship with your son?

The Importance of Fathers

A father's role in the raising of his children has changed dramatically over the past century or two. In previous generations, sons were expected to follow in their fathers' footsteps, apprenticing in their work and in their approaches to life. During the nineteenth century, however, fathers began to go out to work, and the measure of a man's success slowly changed. Rather than the closeness of his family and the strength of his family business, a man's worth could be measured by his income, the value of his house, and the size of his car. Parenting became "women's work"; fathers were just too busy earning a living. And from then on, generations of boys grew up hungering for closeness with a father they barely knew, someone who came home only to eat dinner, look over homework, hear about the day's misbehavior, and watch a little television.

Ross Parke, PhD, at the University of California at Riverside, found that fathers are just as good at reading a baby's emotional cues as mothers are, but they respond in different ways. A father's active play and stimulation may actually help a baby learn to be aware of his own internal state and to tolerate a wide range of people and activities.

Research shows that without a doubt, fathers are an integral part in their sons' healthy emotional, physical, and cognitive growth from their first moments of life. Boys whose fathers love them and can demonstrate that love in consistent, caring ways have fewer problems later in life with peers, academics, and delinquent behavior. One study tracked a group of boys and girls for twenty-six years, exploring the roles of both mothers and fathers in nurturing emotional health and empathy. While the mother's role was important, by far the most influential factor in a child's emotional health was how involved the *father* was in a child's care. In fact, the benefits of having an active, involved father during infancy and early childhood appear to last well into adolescence.

Despite this fact, some fathers don't always know how to connect with their sons. As Dan Kindlon, PhD, and Michael Thompson, PhD, report in *Raising Cain*, ". . . they find it difficult to think in terms of 'love' or to express the love they do feel for a son. Instead, they tend to fall back on what they have been taught to do with other men—namely, compete, control, and criticize."

As boys reach adolescence, their inborn drive to individuate, to become independent people, may lead them to compete and argue with their fathers. Fathers often react by trying to control their sons' opinions and actions, causing conflict. As your boy grows, remember, his task is to become himself, and he needs your support and understanding.

In one study, male executives and managers were asked what single thing they would have changed about their childhood relationships with their fathers. Most of these successful men answered that they wished they had enjoyed a closer relationship with their fathers, and that their dads had been able to express more warmth and emotion.

Showing Affection

Many truly loving dads feel a bit uneasy about showing affection to their young sons. Moms are usually comfortable hugging and cuddling, but fathers, who may never have enjoyed an openly loving relationship with their own fathers (and may not be emotionally literate themselves), often hesitate to show affection and warmth in overt, physical ways. Love need not be expressed only in the verbal, huggy-kissy ways that some moms choose. There are many ways a father can demonstrate his love for his son, and it's important that he do so as often as possible.

TAKE TIME TO PLAY

Spending time together just listening, laughing, and hanging out may be one of the best ways to build a strong bond with your growing son. You can crawl around on the floor with the farm animals and cars when he's a toddler; you can read together, build castles out of blocks, or teach him your favorite sport as he grows. You can wrestle, tickle, bounce, and run. And when your son is a teenager, you can share your passion for rebuilding classic cars, music, fly fishing, or almost anything else. You can certainly invite your son to share the activities you enjoy, but take time to notice what he loves, and find ways to join in with him. You may talk and laugh; you may do some serious listening. But you will be able to connect just by sharing the same space for a while.

Of course, for busy fathers with many responsibilities, finding hangout time can be a challenge. If you consider that your presence in your son's life increases his chances of being successful and happy (and decreases the risk of problem behaviors), you may well decide that there is no higher priority.

It's wonderful to share activities with your boy. Be careful, however, that you don't turn those shared times into unwanted lessons and lectures. Allow your son to learn at his own pace; focus on your relationship with him rather than on how well he is performing a certain task. Encouragement and connection will earn you a companion for life.

DADS AND NONVERBAL LOVE

There is another way that fathers can connect and show warmth and caring to their sons, a way that requires no words at all. Imagine Sam, who is the father of an eleven-year-old boy named Brad. Sam was in the kitchen fixing a snack when Brad came through the front door. Brad didn't meet his dad's gaze and appeared dejected and discouraged. When he reached the comfortable old sofa in the den, he simply fell onto it, closed his eyes, and threw an arm over his face. He sighed deeply.

Sam placed a slice of cheese on a cracker. Brad had something going on this afternoon—what was it? And then it struck him. Today was all-star try-outs for Little League. Brad's appearance left his dad with no doubt about the results: Sam knew Brad had been practicing hard, but there were a lot of talented kids trying out. Sam sighed and swallowed the disappointment he felt on his son's behalf. Then he put a few more slices of cheese and crackers on a plate and carried them into the den with a cold glass of lemonade.

Without a word, he placed the drink and the plate of snacks in front of Brad and sat down next to him. Brad glanced up, but the empathy in his father's face was too much for him; he went back to hiding behind his arm, while a tear slowly slid down his cheek. Sam reached out and stroked his son's forehead. He continued gently rubbing Brad's head and neck until his son sighed and sat up.

Brad took a sip of lemonade. "I didn't make the team, Dad," he said quietly.

Sam smiled and put an arm around his son's shoulders. "I know you're disappointed, Brad. But I also know you gave it your best. I know how hard you worked for this." They sat quietly together a little while longer. When Brad straightened up again, Sam smiled. "Have a snack. Then why don't you keep me company out in the garage for a while? I could use your help with that cabinet I'm building."

Sometimes nonverbal ways of communicating love say far more than the most eloquent words, especially to a boy. A warm gaze, gentle touch, and a plate of snacks let Brad know that his dad understood. Sometimes nonverbal expressions open the door for conversation, understanding, and problem solving. If you pay attention to your own feelings and to those of your son, you will be able to find ways to build powerful connections that can last a lifetime.

Using Empathy

One of the earliest lessons baby boys learn about empathy comes through active play with their fathers. Experts theorize that being stimulated in this way allows a baby to be aware of both his father's emotional state ("Is he just playing?" "Is he mad?") and his own ("Am I tired of bouncing?"

"Is this fun?"). Babies can learn to send signals such as crying or pulling away when they need less stimulation. And throughout a boy's life, his father can be one of his best teachers in the art of empathy and emotional connection.

MIRROR, MIRROR, ON THE WALL

Whether you know it or not, if you are a father, every moment of your life with your son is a lesson. You teach him what to do—and what not to do—every time you have a conversation, offer discipline, or spend time playing together. Interestingly enough, even boys without active fathers in their lives appear to master the concept of masculinity as they grow up. After all, their peers and the prevailing culture will take care of that. What they lack is the sort of nurturing and affection that fathers can offer—when they choose.

A 2009 University of Texas study about mothers' attitudes revealed that most moms believe they could do a better job of balancing work and family if Dad provided more help. Moms also said that "work responsibilities" were the biggest obstacle to a dad's success in fathering.

Our cultural stereotype of the strong, silent man can have a crippling effect on a man's ability to offer his son compassion, warmth, and tenderness. Yet that is often exactly what a boy needs from his father. Boys who do best in studies of psychological adjustment are those with warm, loving fathers, fathers who, perhaps ironically, have qualities often thought of as feminine. Boys who do the worst in psychological adjustment are those whose fathers are abusive, overly harsh, or neglectful.

KNOW WHO YOUR SON IS

When you're a father, it's tempting to focus on behavior, teaching lessons, and encouraging your son to achieve success (or at least to stay out of trouble). Certainly providing discipline, setting reasonable limits, and following through are important parts of fatherhood. No one, however, can nurture empathy and emotional literacy in your son as well as you can.

> True empathy means understanding the feelings and internal experiences of another person. It involves awareness of not only what that person is doing or feeling but also who that person truly is.

One gift a father can give his son is unconditional acceptance and understanding. (This is not always easy, especially when your son turns out to have dreams very different from your own.) Another gift is the truth about your own feelings and experience. When you express your feelings clearly, simply, and in nonthreatening ways, your son has the opportunity to learn from your feelings and his own.

Simply put, your son needs calm, clear information about what you think and feel. You can say, "I'm pretty angry at you right now" instead of yelling. You can say, "I'm disappointed because I didn't get the promotion I wanted" instead of stalking off to the garage alone. When you demonstrate emotional honesty and empathy, you offer your son the ability to nurture those qualities in himself and to become a stronger, happier man.

Be a Role Model

Think for a moment about your own father. You may not have known him well; you may not have known him at all. Or you may have years of precious memories. What did your father—or your father's absence—teach you about being a man? About values? About love and family? If your memories of your father are troubling ones, how would you change your own past if you had the chance?

The wonderful thing about raising a son is that it allows you both to share the best parts of your own childhood and, perhaps, to give your son the things you never had.

WORK, MONEY, AND VALUES

Children are always making decisions. They watch what happens around them, and then decide what they must do to find belonging and connection. Children do not automatically mimic the behavior and values of their parents; they are thinking, feeling people who must decide for themselves what works in life.

Still, your own choices, actions, and values are the plumb line that your son will use to measure what matters in life. If you work long hours, no matter what your reasons might be, your son will draw conclusions about work, family, and your priorities. If you compete with colleagues, family, and the neighbors to have the biggest house, the nicest boat, and the newest car, your son will decide whether he agrees with you—or not. If you tell your son that you value honesty, but he hears you calling in sick to go skiing or bragging about how you managed to avoid paying taxes, he will make his own decisions about ethics—and about you.

Researchers at UCLA spent four years observing thirty-two families in which both parents worked and there were at least two children. These families, they discovered, were in the same room only 16 percent of the time; in five homes, family members were never in the same room. Only one father spent time with his children on a regular basis.

The best way to learn what your son is deciding about life and how to live it is to spend time listening and building a strong connection with him. Children are gifted observers; they rely far more on nonverbal messages than on words. "Do as I say, not as I do" doesn't work with children (especially not with teenagers). Remember the list of qualities and character attributes that you want for your son? It's wise to stop occasionally and consider whether or not your own behavior and choices are nurturing those qualities. The good news is that mistakes aren't fatal; they are wonderful opportunities to learn.

DEALING WITH MISTAKES

It is inevitable. Even the most loving and committed parent loses his temper, makes poor choices, or says hurtful, shaming things. No parent enjoys hurting his child, but what truly matters is what you do *after* a blowup has occurred. In their book *Parenting from the Inside Out*, Daniel J. Siegel, MD, and Mary Hartzell, MEd, put it this way: "Although ruptures of various sorts may be unavoidable, being aware of them is essential before a parent can restore a collaborative, nurturing connection with the child. This reconnecting process can be called repair . . . Ruptures without repair lead to a deepening sense of disconnection between parent and child."

It is important to accept that your son is not responsible for mending the ruptures in your relationship: Repair always begins with the parents. While it may not be easy to admit your own mistakes, accept that you are human, or take responsibility for lost tempers and wrong choices, this, too, is part of being a role model for your son. He wants to know that you are capable and competent so that he can believe in his own capability and competence. But he also needs to know that it is okay to admit mistakes, to take personal responsibility while still accepting himself, and to say "I was wrong" when it is appropriate to do so. Ruptures can actually make relationships stronger and closer when parent and child—father and son—learn to forgive, find solutions, and reconnect.

Being a Connected Father

Michael Gurian, family therapist and author of numerous books on boys, shares an old Turkish saying: "You are not an adult until you have had a child." In many cultures, having and raising children is the mark of a mature human being, and setting aside one's personal needs and ambitions for the welfare and happiness of children is unquestioned. Says Gurian, "I studied thirty cultures and could not find a single one where children are more profoundly lonely than in America. Simultaneously, our adults seem the loneliest, too. In my studies, I found that American parents . . . were the most likely to want to absorb their child into their busy lives and the least likely to say they would give up their busy lives for their child."

No one is suggesting that you sacrifice your own life and dreams for your son. But if you take a moment to look deep inside, you may discover that your son is not the only one who craves connection; fathers do, too. Your son needs your guidance and encouragement in mastering the skills of maturity and in learning to be honest, empathic, and aware. From his first finger-painting to his first job, he will seek your approval in everything he does (whether he shows it or not). Your boy is exquisitely attuned to what you think of him—or what he believes you think of him. Even his misbehavior is designed to get your attention and to provoke a reaction.

But being a conscious, connected, and loving father will enrich your life as well. Your son can teach you curiosity; he can show you how to appreciate the wings of a moth or the usefulness of mud. He can open your mind to new worlds and ideas, if you will let him—and if you can let go of your own beliefs and busyness for just a moment or two. Your son can teach you about wonder, imagination, and heartbreak, all in a single afternoon. The time you spend just being your son's dad may be the wisest investment you ever make, in his life and in your own.

Important Points to Consider

Boys and their fathers share a special relationship. Here are some important points about boys and their dads:

- Though the role of fathers has changed drastically in recent years, many dads do not realize the importance of bonding with their sons.

- Physical and emotional connection is a must for dads and sons. Remember the importance of play in your relationship as well as the subtler ways you can express love for your son.

- As the adult, you must be the one to try and fix ruptures in your relationship with your son. Everyone makes mistakes in parenting;

make sure you admit when you have done wrong and take responsibility for mending your relationship.

O Fathers often serve as the earliest role models for their sons' behavior. You must make sure that you are practicing what you preach in your own life if you expect your son to do the same.

 **CHAPTER 8**

Boys and Moms

Boys need their mothers' love. They also need the freedom to begin their own journeys through life. Mothers are parents, first and foremost. But mothers also share something very special with their growing boys. No matter how much time may stretch and bend your relationship with your son, and despite the occasional arguments and silences, your son yearns for your unconditional love and support. He can step into his own life with courage when he carries your love forever in his heart. As a mom you must find the balance between nurturing your son and encouraging independence and confidence.

Finding a Balance

A little boy's relationship with his mother is usually his first experience of intimacy. She feeds him from her breast, rocks him to sleep, and appears by his crib when he cries in the night. As he learns to walk, it is usually his mother who provides the safe place from which he ventures out to explore his world and who cuddles him warmly when he returns.

Yet when her son approaches adolescence, a mother begins to receive subtle signals that it's time to let go. No more public hugs; touch becomes something that must be carefully monitored. Well-meaning mothers, worried about smothering their growing boys, may withdraw from their sons, leaving them to the world of men and the myths of masculinity. It is a loss—and an unnecessary one—for both mothers and sons.

Boys, too, feel pressure to put some emotional distance between themselves and their mothers. After all, who hasn't heard the dreaded epithets *mama's boy*, *sissy*, and *tied to the apron strings*? American culture places a high premium on self-sufficiency and strength in its males, discouraging emotional awareness and expression. And it is assumed that girls (and moms) are emotional; in order to find a place as healthy men, the reasoning goes, boys must separate themselves from their mothers.

Imagine Stephen, who is fourteen years old. He loves football, video games, books, and a good joke, and he shares all of these interests with his mom, Jackie. When asked, Stephen says readily that he loves his mom. She has raised him alone, and he respects and appreciates her hard work, generosity, and unfailing support for him. When they are alone, Stephen loves to read side by side with his mom and to have her scratch his back. He always gives her a hug before he heads to his room at night.

Things change when his friends come around, however. When he leaves the house these days, he restricts himself to scowling at his mom and saying gruffly, "See you later, Mom." When Jackie comes too close or tells him to be safe, he rolls his eyes at his friends. "I know it hurts her feelings. I feel bad sometimes," he says. "But it's embarrassing to say 'I love you.' She should know that by now."

Chances are that later on, when the chaos and confusion of adolescence have passed, Stephen will feel more comfortable showing affection for his mother, even when his friends are present. For now, however, like most young men, his dignity depends on keeping his distance.

Raising a son means finding the balance between opposing forces: closeness and distance, support and letting go, kindness and firmness. Mothers can certainly learn how to provide both love and structure and to teach the skills a boy will need to become mature. Love, however, is a necessary part of parenting, and the special bond that many mothers share with their sons is an asset, not a liability. Mothers can teach their boys how to love fully and freely. Through conscious parenting, they offer their sons their first lessons in the power of connection.

What Sons Learn from Their Mothers

Boys learn their earliest lessons about love and trust from their mothers. According to William Pollack, PhD, "far from making boys weaker, the love of a mother can and does actually make boys stronger, emotionally and psychologically. Far from making boys dependent, the base of safety a loving mother can create—a connection that her son can rely on all his life—provides a boy with the courage to explore the outside world. But most important, far from making a boy act in 'girl-like' ways, a loving mother actually plays an integral role in helping a boy develop his masculinity."

THE IMPORTANCE OF A LOVING REFUGE

In the early years of a little boy's life, he is torn between two choices: He longs to explore, climb, jump, and run, and he needs to stay close to the adults who allow him to feel secure. In fact, when boys begin to walk and exercise some autonomy, their activity mirrors this dual need. They wander away from Mom (into the backyard, across the playground, or to the neighbor's house) and then return for a quick conversation or a hug, just to be sure she's there.

Your son will learn self-respect and confidence when you provide a loving, secure, and understanding home base for him. When you create a sense of belonging and significance for your boy, teach him life and character skills, and practice kind, firm discipline, he learns to trust, face challenges, and move freely into his world. When you take time to listen to him and to focus on solutions to the problems he faces, you teach him emotional awareness and good judgment. A strong and loving relationship with a good mother can help a boy learn the skills of intimacy, support him in developing respect for other women, and prepare him for a satisfying relationship with a partner someday.

Some mothers, absorbing cultural messages about *real masculinity*, believe that they should push their sons away emotionally, often as early as the age of two or three. Your son needs consistent connection with you all the way through adolescence. Be sensitive about invading privacy, but separating yourself from your son will do him more harm than good.

KNOWING WHEN TO LET GO

Even the wisest mother can find it hard to let go in appropriate ways when her son begins to exercise his independence. Your son's desire to do things for himself, from dressing himself to reading his own bedtime story to dating, can feel like a personal rejection. One of the paradoxes of parenting is that if you do your job as a mother well, your son will eventually leave you.

As your son grows, you will learn to find the balance between offering support and stepping back to let him learn from his own experiences—and his own mistakes. Clinging too tightly can create unnecessary power struggles, especially during adolescence (a rather bumpy period for even the closest mothers and sons). Teach skills and listen well and often; then have faith in your son and let go.

Connecting with Your Son

Fathers usually build relationships with their sons through active play and stimulation; they "do stuff" together. For mothers and boys, the process may be a little different. The bond between a mother and son often grows out of simply spending time together. From infancy into childhood and adolescence, a good mother is just there. Boys often say that their mom is the one person who understands them. That understanding usually grows out of the hours spent offering undivided attention, responding to signals and cues, and providing comfort, support, and encouragement.

SELF-AWARENESS FOR MOMS

You may have grown up with brothers, active boys who are a part of your childhood memories. Or you may have had sisters (or no siblings at all), and boys seem like beings from another planet. You may have an intimate, loving marriage, or you may be deeply disappointed in your partner. You may even be a single mom for one of many reasons.

Many women are surprised to discover that their own experiences with men color their relationships with their sons. If men have caused you pain or you do not trust them, you may find it difficult to relax with your son, to enjoy him, and to allow him to be an active, happy little boy. Your attitudes will unconsciously affect your son's beliefs about his own maleness, perhaps in ways that are not in his best interest—or yours.

Behaviors that make boys different from girls, such as impulsivity, risk-taking, silence, and anger, are often behaviors that mothers struggle with. After all, they didn't do those things when they were kids! Take time to learn all you can about boys and your boy in particular. Get to know the parents and caregivers of other boys and don't be afraid to talk to your son about how he views himself. Understanding will help you choose your battles and set reasonable limits.

Part of being a conscious parent is being in touch with your deepest self. Awareness of your own attitudes toward men and boys will help you connect more easily with your son. Whether you express them openly or not, your beliefs about men will influence your son's feelings about himself. It may be wise to seek out a skilled therapist to help you resolve your own past so that you can build a strong, loving bond with your son.

SKILLS FOR CONNECTING WITH YOUR SON

There is an old saying that you can judge a man's worth as a spouse by the quality of his relationship with his mother. And in fact, a boy's bond with his mother is one of the deepest, most enduring relationships he will experience in his lifetime. It should also be one of the healthiest and most supportive. Here are some suggestions for building a strong, loving connection with your boy:

O **Listen and observe.** Good mothers are willing to spend time just listening and watching. Be accepting of how your son reacts based on his unique traits. Ask curiosity questions to draw your son out; let him finish his thoughts before offering suggestions or advice.

O **Spend time just being together.** Relationships require time. You must be willing to hang out, play, and do things face to face with your son. Carve out at least fifteen minutes a day that belong just to your boy—no multitasking allowed!

O **Respond to your son's cues.** When he says, "I can do it myself, Mom!" teach the necessary skills, be sure he's safe, and then allow him to try. It is skills and experience that build self-esteem.

O **Be curious about his interests.** If your son loves an activity, sharing his enthusiasm is a wonderful way to build connection. Watch his favorite sport with him; admire the new skateboard tricks he learns. Understanding your son's world will keep you connected.

O **Know his friends.** There is no better way to learn about your son than to watch him at play with his friends. As your son grows, welcome his friends into your home. If he can bring his life to you, he is less likely to feel the need to hide it from you.

○ **Respect his privacy.** Even little boys need time to themselves. Your son may choose to play alone in his room from time to time, or to disappear into his computer or stereo headphones. You can show him that you care and still respect his need for private space.

○ **Provide kind, firm discipline and don't be afraid to follow through.** "Wait 'til your father gets home" doesn't work. Learn effective discipline skills; then be willing to set limits and follow through.

○ **Be sensitive about touch, especially in public.** Hugs are wonderful, but some touch may make your son uncomfortable, especially as he gets older. You may want to have a family rule that bathrooms and bedrooms (yours and his) are private spaces and cannot be entered without knocking. Respecting his needs will keep the connection between you relaxed and open.

Boys need connection with their mothers. If the outside world does not intrude, most are happy to stay close and connected for most of their growing-up years. Your knowledge of your son will help you know when he welcomes a hug and when he does not. It is a delicate balancing act, but time and love will teach you how to stay connected to your boy at the same time that you encourage him to exercise his independence.

Making Room for Growth

A loving mother can provide a safe, secure base from which her son ventures forth to explore his world. Sometimes, though, even the most sensitive and caring mother can have trouble letting go. Your relationship with your son needs to breathe; that is, there needs to be room for both of you to come together and then move gently apart. You will need time and space to care for yourself and to nurture your adult relationships; your boy will need room to become confident and independent.

Truly loving your son means teaching him the skills and attitudes he needs to eventually leave you. As your son establishes an independent life, however, you will know that you taught him to strike out on his own and become a healthy, confident young man. Independence does not mean the end of love and connection; it simply marks a new phase of your relationship with your son.

As time passes, your son will begin to move away from you, spending time with new friends and new activities. Nurturing your own physical, emotional, and spiritual health is an essential ingredient in raising your son. He needs to know that Mom has a life and he is free to live his own.

OTHER RELATIONSHIPS

As your son grows, he will develop new friendships and relationships outside your family. Some of these friendships, especially as he enters adolescence, will not include you—at least not directly. A wise mom understands that she will not remain number one in her son's life forever. Other relationships—with friends and, perhaps, with romantic partners—will become increasingly important as your son matures.

Your ability to listen will serve you well as your son builds a life of his own. There is an old saying that if you truly love something, you must set it free. So it is with your growing boy; he will gladly stay connected to you when you can open your hand and allow him to fly on his own.

The Importance of Play

Mothers like words. Moms talk a lot, express emotions verbally, and rely on language to build connection and closeness. But boys sometimes have a different style. While you can teach your son emotional literacy, you may discover that he is most comfortable speaking the language of action. In other words, you may be able to connect best with your son by doing things with him.

To understand how to play with your son, think of Veronica, a busy mom for whom there were never enough hours in the day. Veronica's four-year-old son, Clint, had his own way of letting his mom know when he was feeling neglected: He misbehaved. When Veronica got too caught up in work, community activities, or household projects, Clint simply dug in his heels and refused to cooperate. A tantrum usually ensued.

One evening Veronica went looking for her son to begin his bedtime routine. Sure enough, there he was in front of the television, playing his favorite video game. He looked up at her and scowled, and then returned to his game. Veronica bit back the reprimand that sprang to her lips, choosing instead to settle on the floor next to Clint.

"What are you playing, Clint?" she asked him.

Clint gave her a slightly suspicious look. "You have to race these cars around, and you get points for crashing them," he explained. Then he hesitated. "Do you want to play, Mom?" he asked.

"Well, I don't know how, but I can try," Veronica said, picking up a controller and frowning at the buttons.

Of course, Clint promptly whomped his mom at the car-crashing game—three straight times. Veronica gave up, laughing, and pulled Clint into her lap for a hug. "I'm terrible at that game!" she exclaimed.

"Well, I could teach you," Clint offered, looking shyly up at his mom. "Then we could play together sometimes."

Veronica recognized that her little boy was offering to share a part of his life with her. "I'd like that," she said.

There is a time and place for words; in fact, by using the language of feelings, mothers can help their sons learn to be more comfortable with emotions. Boys will not always want to talk, however, especially when they're hurt or sad. Sometimes, it is the silent spaces in a relationship that speak most clearly.

Sure enough, at four o'clock the next afternoon, Clint bounded into the kitchen and announced, "Mom, it's time for your video-game lesson!"

Clint was delighted to be the expert for once, and Veronica discovered that while she'd never love video games, she thoroughly enjoyed the time she spent laughing and playing with her son on his turf.

Playing together turned out to be a marvelous way to avoid tantrums; Clint felt connected to his mom, and Veronica got to learn about her son. It was a win-win solution.

What your son needs most from you is the knowledge that you are there when he needs you, a safe harbor to return to in a storm. He also needs to know that you have faith in him—in his abilities, his character, and the person he is becoming. By sharing your son's activities and interests, you send him the message that you care about what he cares about. Sure, you may not be able to join the football team with him, but you can find ways to support his interests. Simply going for a walk, touring a museum, or even grocery shopping together can provide precious opportunities to connect.

Build Positive Attitudes about Women

As a mother, you are your son's most influential teacher about women. The choices you make will teach your son powerful lessons about his own relationships with women.

Imagine that you are a spectator at a mother-son playgroup, watching the pairs of mothers and sons as they join in various activities. One mother hovers over her son, pulling him back before he can take even the smallest risk. Another mother talks to a friend in the corner, ignoring her son's pleas to "look at me, Mommy." One mother hugs her son every few minutes, while he squirms and struggles to break free. Yet another follows her son around the room, picking up toys, handing him snacks, and making sure he doesn't need to do anything for himself.

All of these boys are making decisions about themselves, about their mothers, and about what they must do to belong and feel valued. They are also learning compelling lessons about women. Take a moment to think: If you wait on your son, clean up after him, and teach him that he is the center of the universe, what is he learning about women? If you insist that your son listen to your problems, carry your emotional burdens, and tell you that you look pretty, what is he learning about women? If you try to hug and touch him constantly and expect him to spend all of his time with you, what is he learning about women?

RESPECT YOUR SON, RESPECT YOURSELF

Perhaps the best way to create a healthy relationship with your son is to practice mutual respect. You should respect your son's individuality, his feelings, and his needs, even when you don't agree with them (or when you need to provide discipline). You should also show respect for yourself. Remember, pampering and permissiveness are not effective parenting styles; your son needs limits and boundaries to become a healthy young adult. When you offer respect to your son and also treat yourself with respect, your son is more likely to respect all of the women he encounters, from his first-grade teacher to his future wife.

Important Points to Consider

Boys share a unique and important relationship with their mothers. Mothers walk a fine line between nurturing and support and building independence in their sons. Being there for your son and allowing him to grow and make mistakes are all part of being a conscious parent. Here are some important points to consider:

- Boys need and appreciate the support and connection that they get from their mothers.

- Women's own experiences with men may color their responses to their son's behavior. It's important to acknowledge and accept this.

- Moms should be just as involved as fathers in healthy, active play with their sons. Play is an important part of how your son will learn.

- Be a role model for your son in how to treat women in his life. Teach your son to build positive attitudes about women by treating yourself with respect.

 **CHAPTER 9**

Friends and Their Influences

Understanding how a boy forms friendships (or fails to) will help you support him as he enters the world of his peers. And it can be a very important world to your son. He may begin with one or two children from the neighborhood or preschool. When his school years begin, he will gravitate toward friends who share his interests. And by the time he is in high school, friends will have all but eclipsed parents in importance. Problems will invariably arise, but it is rarely helpful to intervene in your son's friendships. Instead, focus on understanding your son's feelings and perhaps helping him find solutions to his problems. Your son's friends are not competition for his love and loyalty. By making room for your boy to love his friends and by teaching him how to be a good friend, you ensure that the bond between you will stay healthy and strong.

Developing Social Skills

Children aren't born with social skills. While your son is an infant, he is preoccupied with learning how to operate his body, building a connection with you, and finding ways to communicate. Babies are not able to recognize the pudgy figure in the mirror as "me" until they are about one year old; not surprisingly, their abilities to relate to others take a while to develop. At first, your son will simply play next to other children, and he won't particularly care who they are. But as he becomes more aware (usually around the age of two or three), he will begin to experiment with relationships. Not all of these experiments turn out well.

THE LABORATORY OF PLAY

Play is truly how a young child learns about his world. He explores, shakes, pokes, and pulls. He grabs and climbs. Unfortunately, when the object of all this activity is another child, scrapes, bumps, and hurt feelings can result. Young children have not yet learned how to share; the idea of playing cooperatively takes some getting used to. A preschooler sees himself as the central figure in his own world, and making room for others takes time and practice.

By the age of two or three, gender differences appear in the ways children conduct their friendships. Girls often prefer one or two best friends and build intense relationships with them. Boys tend to gather groups of friends, playing less intensely with more people. Boys may express anger through physical aggression, while girls fight with snubs, rumors, and insults.

"NO ONE WILL PLAY WITH ME!"

Some children seem to be born with the gift of charm. They make friends easily, are comfortable with new people and situations, and know just how to wriggle their way into a new group of children. Others, however, hang back, cling to parents, and struggle to gain admittance to games and conversations. It is heartbreaking to watch a child sit all alone or to hear him say sadly, "Nobody likes me."

A child's success in the world of his peers depends in part on his ability to send and receive accurate nonverbal signals. For instance, a child who stands too close to others, talks too loudly, dresses strangely, or touches too often will find it difficult to fit in. Other children appear angry when they don't intend to or do not know how to join a game already in progress.

Researchers now believe that shyness may be genetically influenced; in other words, some people are shy for life. Rather than pushing your child to do something he finds difficult or discouraging, accept his temperament, focus on teaching him coping skills, and be patient as he learns.

The good news about most social skills is that they can be taught—and learned. If you can, find an opportunity to observe your boy with other children and see what happens. Preschool staff and teachers may also be able to keep a kind eye on your son and let you know why he is struggling to make friends. Kind, gentle encouragement and opportunities to practice will often solve the problem.

Boys and Their Friends

Boys and girls crave connection and belonging. Like all of us, boys need friends, suffer when they believe they don't have any, and agonize over the ups and downs of relationships. Many adults believe that somehow boys need friends less than girls do; the myth of the stoic male has intruded even into childhood. In truth, though, no boy is an island; boys value their friends throughout childhood and adolescence and are happier and healthier when they have solid relationships with peers.

ACTION, NOT WORDS

Despite the common belief that girls are better at relationships, most boys consider their friends a vital part of their lives. Boys may actually be better at maintaining friendships than girls are; a recent study of ten- to fifteen-year-old boys and girls found that girls' friendships are actually more fragile. Girls tend to say and do hurtful things to each other more frequently than boys, and girls are more hurt by the end of a friendship.

Be cautious about signing up your son for daily groups and activities. Experts warn that overscheduling children deprives them of the opportunity to learn to entertain themselves. If you insist on too many sports, playgroups, and other activities, your son may be unable to simply play in the backyard.

Boys' friendships are usually built around active play. Boys are the living definition of the phrase *peer group*; they love games with rules, competition, and doing things together. Boys' play usually includes a fair amount of teasing, some of which can occasionally veer off into meanness, especially if they perceive another boy as weak or clumsy. Boys seem to enjoy the opportunity to test themselves against others, and many lasting friendships begin in karate class or on the basketball court. Competence and skill are widely respected; being picked last for a team or left out altogether is an experience that can haunt a boy for years.

TEENS AND FRIENDSHIP

As boys mature, friendships become even more important, and they frequently widen to include girls. During the teen years, friends can become the most important part of a boy's life—and a part from which he excludes his parents. Many parents discover that the exuberant boy who used to welcome them into his life with open arms becomes intensely private, even exclusive, during adolescence. Your son will always need connection, but now, in addition to connection with you, he needs connection with a group of friends who understand him, accept him, and share his perspective on the world.

The turbulence and confusion of being a teenager leads boys to form close bonds with friends. Underneath the incessant teasing and joking, there is the sense for many boys that a friend is someone who is "always there for me," someone he can trust implicitly. They may be partners in crime (and the occasional party) or partners in study, but friendships between adolescent boys can run surprisingly deep.

You may feel a bit left out, even hurt, by the intensity of your son's involvement with and loyalty to his friends during his teen years. Chances are good that he will not talk to you as openly; after all, one of the tasks of adolescence is building an identity that is separate from parents. Pushing your son to talk, open up, share details of his personal life, or include you in his activities usually makes matters worse. Patience, reasonable limits, and respect are key ingredients in consciously parenting your teen son.

Though your son's relationships with friends can be turbulent, it is unwise to intervene. Instead, coach your son in the skills he will need to repair his relationships. Encourage him to take responsibility for his behavior, understand his friends' feelings, and look for ways to make situations better. It's better to offer empathy than unwanted advice.

Sports and Emotional Expression

Not all boys love sports or want to play them; there are lots of healthy, happy boys who prefer music, art, or science. Still, many boys participate in organized sports and competition at some point in their lives, and for many, sports define the way they see themselves and are a path to belonging and significance. Sports can build a connection between a parent and son, and provide a comfortable arena in which to explore pride, disappointment, determination, and even defeat. Sports can allow boys to learn about themselves and to form close friendships with others. Or sports can cause a boy to feel humiliation, embarrassment, and shame.

Americans love sports, largely because they are a metaphor for the struggles in life we all share. For boys, sports can provide something they may not find anywhere else in their young lives: a safe place to have feelings. With the right coaching and parental support, sports allow boys to work hard, learn about themselves, risk failure, and experience the joy of accomplishing something in the company of others. Many boys never forget the season they went undefeated, their first birdie on the golf course, or that personal best in swimming.

What if your son wants to quit a sport and try a new one? Boys aren't always sure they will really like something they sign up for. Decide what you want your son to learn from a sport. Then sit and talk together about following through. Boys need to be able to try new activities, and parents need to accept this and recognize that not everything will be a good fit.

IT'S ONLY A GAME

It is wonderful when parents can share a boy's dream, support him in his efforts, and provide encouragement. It is harmful when parents push too hard. Your son should play because *he* wants to; it's as simple as that.

You should also be sure to pay attention at practice and games. Most coaches are involved in sports because they care about young people and want to help them. Some, however, believe that shaming and humiliating boys is acceptable if it leads to victory. While some teasing is part of the process, never allow your son to be mistreated physically or verbally by coaches or teammates.

Even if you cannot closely observe how the coach or other players treat your son, there are other ways for you to tell if the sport is a good fit for your child. You may find your boy waiting by the car with all his equipment half an hour before each practice. Or he may develop a stomachache and refuse to talk before and after practices. Be patient and take time to listen. He may have good reason for his feelings.

Remember that your son's worth does not depend on his athletic accomplishments. No matter how hard they work and practice, most boys will never be professional athletes. Notice your son's effort and improvement; be gentle with his faults and failures. Constant criticism of his play will not make him love sports—or you. Your son can learn a great deal about life, determination, and teamwork from sports, and he'll learn best if you help him remember that it truly is only a game.

The Harmful Lack of Play

Japanese photographer Keiki Haginoya began a project during the 1970s to document the play of children on the streets of Tokyo. The project was intended to last a lifetime, but it ended in 1996; the photographer could no longer find children playing in the streets and vacant lots of the city to photograph.

Children no longer play the way they used to, and in an effort to accommodate the academic demands of No Child Left Behind, and the focus of standardized testing to measure student success, many U.S. schools have eliminated recess from the daily schedule—not a good thing for active boys. In addition, many parents are too worried to allow their children to play outdoors or to roam their neighborhoods unsupervised.

A University of Michigan study found that from 1979 to 1999, children lost an average of twelve hours of free time each week, including eight hours of unstructured play. Most of this time was lost to organized sports and activities and video or online play. It is safe to assume that children have lost even more free time since this study was performed.

Why does this matter? Children learn surprising lessons from play, especially play with peers. They learn the skills of compromise and negotiation; they learn to wait their turn and to accept being "out" when they lose. They create games with elaborate rules and stay physically active and alert. As unstructured play has disappeared, many children are no longer learning these important lessons about getting along with others. In fact, bullying has increased as the amount of free play has decreased.

Bullying and Boys

Each day, as many as 160,000 children stay home from school. They aren't sick, although they may claim to be. They are afraid. Bullying is a problem of global proportions, and intervention programs exist in almost every country to deal with children who hurt other children. Still, almost every child can tell stories about watching a bully at work, being bullied himself, or participating in some way in bullying another child. Why this epidemic of violence and aggression?

WHAT BULLYING LOOKS LIKE

Bullying is about power. The days when the local tough kid grabbed some milk money and gave its former owner a black eye are largely past, although physical bullying still occurs. Bullying these days is often subtler.

Bullies usually target children they perceive as unlikely to fight back. A child may become the target of a bully because of his appearance, economic level, ethnicity, or speech. Bullies have become more creative in the ways they inflict pain and shame on their victims: They may use insults, racial slurs, or other verbal taunts to humiliate other children. They may use emotional or relational bullying, such as excluding their targets from lunch or play. Or they may use technology.

CYBERBULLYING

In just a few short years, sophisticated technology has given bullies some powerful new weapons. Kids can now use cell phones with built-in cameras, computers, social networks, and sophisticated software to attack, shame, and humiliate their targets, sometimes with an online audience of hundreds. Numerous studies have documented a connection between cyberbullying and depression and suicidal thoughts.

Be aware that there may be far more going on in your son's world than you know. Learn Internet safety yourself and invite your boy to talk with you often about his life online.

WHY BOYS BECOME BULLIES

A surprising number of boys have themselves participated in bullying—a fact many of their parents would be dismayed to learn. Many bullies have been bullied themselves, sometimes by their own parents. Remember, where there is behavior, there is an underlying cause. Ridicule, overly harsh teasing, or neglect may spur a boy to take out his own pain on those around him. A bully may hurt others because he feels insecure or has suffered a trauma he finds impossible to talk about.

Still, there is no excuse for deliberately causing pain. Conscious parents can prevent bullying by making time for connection, by showing boys how to manage anger and use words to express emotions, and by setting clear limits about hurting others. Schools can help by having class meetings to discuss bullying, shaming, and teasing. Research shows that schools with active, involved principals and trained teachers experience less bullying.

IS YOUR SON A TARGET?

Many boys suffer at the hands of a bully at least once or twice during their school years. Here are warning signals that your son may be the target of a bully:

○ **Feigning illness.** A child who is being bullied often develops stomachaches or headaches each morning before school or comes home "sick" before recess or lunch.

○ **Avoiding school.** A boy who used to love school may begin crying, begging to stay home, or even inventing school holidays.

○ **Changing habits.** You may notice that your son has nightmares or can't fall asleep. He may eat less or spend hours alone in his room. He may refuse to go outside to play or begin walking blocks out of his way to and from school or the bus stop.

○ **Losing focus.** Your son may have trouble paying attention at school, remembering assignments, or doing his homework. He may seem distracted and spacey.

If your son is being picked on by a bully, he needs your unconditional support and love. Being bullied often causes a boy to lose a great deal of self-respect and confidence. Create opportunities to listen; let him know about the changes you have observed in his attitude and behavior. You can ask gentle "what" and "how" questions to learn more about his day. For example, you might ask, "What happened on the way to school today?" or "You seem quiet and sad; how can I help?" You can also ask your son's teacher to pay extra attention to recess, lunchtime, and hallway behavior and to let you know what she notices.

Be sure that you do not unintentionally encourage bullying behavior by presenting your son with role models who glorify aggression. A bully is not strong or manly. Real men do not need to inflict pain on others to feel secure and confident.

It may be tempting to encourage your son to fight back against a bully, but retaliation rarely solves the problem. Still, no one has the right to hurt your son. You may be able to coach him in keeping his temper, using humor to defuse the situation, walking away confidently, or asking a friend to walk with him when the bully is around. Some bullying situations require adult intervention, however. Be sure you work with your son to make a plan.

Friendships with Girls

Most little boys begin life with few prejudices about gender. They're happy to play with anyone who wants to do what they do. As boys grow a little older, however, they begin to be more aware that girls are just, well, different. Their bodies and voices are different; they like different games and toys. By the age of five or six, many boys have become painfully aware that boys are supposed to act like boys—strong, unafraid, and independent. These are the years when a boy's room is likely to sport a banner declaring, "No girls allowed!"

CHANGING ATTITUDES ABOUT GIRLS

Part of the reason boys avoid girls (at least when their friends are around) during the growing-up years is because they are beginning to be aware of sexuality. Little boys learn about biology and bodies much earlier these days than used to be the case; they are both attracted by and curious about the little girls they know. If they play with girls, they may open themselves up to teasing about being in love ("Roy and Alice sitting in a tree, k-i-s-s-i-n-g . . ."), or even about being gay. Many little boys find it easier to avoid girls altogether—even the girls they may have played with happily when they were younger.

By the time a boy reaches the age of ten or eleven, however, his curiosity is beginning to outweigh his suspicion. Boys have feelings, too, remember, and girls often make good friends. By the time early adolescence has rolled around, boys begin to view girls as potential friends, as well as dates.

GIRL FRIENDS VERSUS GIRLFRIENDS

Friendships between boys and girls may widen a boy's emotional repertoire and allow him to experience talking freely about his life for the first time. Friendship with girls may be a boy's first encounter with emotional intimacy and trust. Sexual curiosity plays a role, too, and not surprisingly, boys are often reluctant to discuss these complex friendships with parents.

You can help your son form healthy friendships with girls by being neither too pushy ("Oh, your girlfriend is so cute! Would you like me to drive you to the movies?") or too discouraging ("You're way too young to be spending time with girls. Where's your football?") Listen well, encourage respect, and focus on the attitudes you want your son to learn. No one can have too many good friends, regardless of their gender.

Supporting Your Son's Friendships

Every parent dreads watching a boy struggle with friendships—and most do at some time during their lives. Your son may tell you, "No one will play with me" or "Everyone's invited to Sandy's party except me." Parents sometimes have a hard time knowing when to try to help and when to back off.

Like it or not, you cannot choose your son's friends for him. Nor does rushing to the rescue when he argues with friends or feels lonely teach him the skills he needs to learn. Your son will undoubtedly bring home friends whom you do not like from time to time. Forbidding him to see them usually makes them more attractive. Instead, invite your son's friends to your home, where you can observe, model good values yourself, and focus on teaching your son about respect, limits, and character.

Friends are a vital and important part of your son's life. You can support him best by offering him opportunities to meet and connect with friends, by allowing him to learn through experience, and by trusting your boy to build respectful friendships with boys and girls. When your son's friendships hit bumpy spots (and they will), don't rush to intervene or rescue him. Instead, listen, invite him to talk about his feelings and actions, and focus on teaching character and skills.

Important Points to Consider

Your son's friendships will play a major role in his life. And while it is wise to let your son handle his friendships independently, be ready to listen to your son when he comes to you with friendship issues. As a conscious parent, you can always be there to offer advice or empathy without interfering. Encouraging your son's friendships will help him grow as a person. Here are some important points regarding his interaction with peers:

- Parents are the first models for appropriate social interaction.

- Boys' early friendships are often built around active play.

- Involvement in sports is a great way to get physically fit and develop social skills. However, not all boys view sports and competition the same way, and some will need support and guidance from their parents.

- Many boys become targets of bullies—or become bullies themselves. Explaining acceptable behavior and modeling empathy can minimize the effect of bullying.

- A boy's friendships with girls are important to developing emotional maturity. Parents can allow for the healthy development of these relationships by not being too pushy and being there to help their son navigate this new territory.

**CHAPTER 10**

Your Adolescent Son

When a boy becomes a teenager, parents often believe that he will need less hands-on parenting. Actually, teenagers need active, connected parents just as much as younger boys do, but the relationship must change a bit to make room for a teen's growing independence. Indeed, your son will change dramatically during his teen years, physically, emotionally, and sexually. Excessive control will create power struggles; permissiveness is dangerous. Your son needs kind, firm, conscious parenting and reasonable limits more than ever before.

Understanding Your Adolescent

Teens are not just defiant almost-adults; they are also idealistic, thoughtful, and loyal. As boys make their way through adolescence, they are expected to build independent identities, learn to manage their own lives, and stay out of trouble. Not surprisingly, boys and their parents often find adolescence a bit challenging.

In their book *Positive Discipline for Teenagers*, Jane Nelsen, EdD, and Lynn Lott, MA, MFT, observe that human beings are born twice. The first time, our mothers do the labor. The second time, we do the labor ourselves during adolescence. Nelsen and Lott note, "The second time is often harder on our mothers and us."

Adolescence has long been viewed as a time of intense turmoil and change; the words *rebellious* and *teenager* often appear in the same sentence. Still, awareness and conscious parenting skills will help you keep your connection with your son and allow both of you not only to survive but also to enjoy his teen years.

THE TEENAGE BRAIN

Just as technology has allowed us to understand the brains and development of young children, it has opened a window into the often confusing and tumultuous world of teenagers. Parents are frequently deceived by the mature physical appearance of teens and expect adult thinking and behavior. When teens make mistakes (they will), lose their tempers (they will), or act impulsively (yes, they will do that, too), parents may feel hurt, surprised, and worried. When teens insist on privacy, stop talking about their personal lives, and retreat into their rooms for hours on end, parents may take it personally. If you understand adolescent development, however, you will be better able to stay connected to your son, set reasonable limits, and help him learn self-discipline and life skills.

Research in the past few years has taught us some surprising things about the adolescent brain. Teenagers may look a lot like adults, but their brains are different. And those differences account for many of the characteristics that adults have difficulty understanding. You may remember that during your son's first few years of life, his brain was actively growing, forming new synapses at an amazing pace. Late in childhood, the brain prunes synapses that are not needed. Your son's genes, as well as the experiences he has had growing up, determine which synapses (and how many) will be pruned. Then, just as adolescence begins, the brain experiences another spurt in growth—including the addition of hormones.

THE PREFRONTAL CORTEX

The prefrontal cortex is the part of the brain responsible for executive functions, such skills as impulse control, good judgment, and weighing alternatives—in other words, all the abilities parents wish teenagers had more of. Researchers believe, however, that the prefrontal cortex does not fully mature until a person is around twenty-five years old, largely because the nerves connecting the frontal lobes with the rest of the brain lack a complete coating of myelin and don't send signals efficiently. This helps explain why teens are so likely to be impulsive (accidents are the leading cause of death for teenagers) and so unlikely to consider consequences before acting.

Adolescence may also affect the brain's circadian rhythms. You may have noticed that your son "can't" fall asleep before midnight and then "can't" get up in the morning for class. He may not be avoiding school or defying you; many teens find that their sleep cycle shifts by a couple of hours during adolescence.

Another function of the prefrontal cortex is to help control the emotional centers of the brain. This is where hormones enter the story.

Hormones and Emotions in Adolescence

Emotions are powerful things. All boys struggle from time to time to express their emotions clearly and effectively, but by the teen years, most boys have difficulty showing feelings, asking for help, or even being truly aware of their own emotional states. As if this isn't enough of a challenge, the hormones that accompany the physical changes of adolescence complicate matters even more. Emotions, which often prompt impulsive behavior, are flowing freely, while the part of the brain intended to manage them is not yet mature. No wonder teens and their parents can feel so irritated with each other!

> Hormones (especially testosterone) appear to affect a teen's ability to read nonverbal signals accurately. Adults use the prefrontal cortex to read emotional cues, but teenagers rely on the limbic system, the system responsible for gut feelings. Teen boys often read emotional cues inaccurately. For instance, when shown pictures of adult faces expressing various emotions, adolescent boys interpret most of them as anger.

During your son's teen years it is more important than ever to stay connected, use your listening skills to draw him out, and continue to give him words for his often unruly emotions. As much as possible, remain calm—even when your son is not. (Taking time to cool off is a valuable tool for both teens and parents.) Use active listening skills to help your son identify his own emotions; it may be helpful to share your own feelings as well as experiences you had in your own adolescence. Remember, even though it may feel deeply personal, much of your son's behavior (and anger) is not really about you.

The Journey to Adulthood

Adolescence is a critically important part of healthy human development, but it is rarely simple. Teens have to make sense of several conflicting needs. They want to remain connected to parents and family (although they may not want to admit it). They want adult privileges and opportunities. They may feel anxious about their approaching independence. And they want to fit in with friends, experiment with new behavior, and learn things for themselves. It can all feel overwhelming.

PHYSICAL CHANGES

It is inescapable; during adolescence, your little boy turns into something completely new. He grows taller, his muscles thicken, and his voice deepens. Hair appears in unexpected places—or doesn't, which is equally as confusing. His genitals grow and develop, and he begins to experience new urges and needs. These changes often make a boy uncomfortable with parents—especially with Mom—and lead to an increased desire for privacy.

These outward changes happen at the same time as an important internal change: Your son must begin his journey from childhood to adulthood. This transition is called *individuation*, and it is not always a simple process. Your son must discover his own identity and begin to consider how to live his adult life. He wants to have fun, which may lead him toward risky behavior; his friends have become extremely important in his life. Boys especially may feel pressure to decide on a career path and to be seen as competent and capable. Your son must discover how to separate himself from you, which is why so many formerly compliant children suddenly become allergic to everything their parents believe.

SUPPORTING YOUR SON

Wise parents can be a tremendous help to boys in navigating the turbulent waters of adolescence. Your relationship with your son will change during these years, but it need not become distant or difficult. Here are some suggestions to consider:

- O **Stay connected.** Even if your son claims that he doesn't care if you come to his sports events or school activities, make time to show up. Just knowing you're present and paying attention in his life can make a huge difference.

- O **Remain an active parent who listens.** Your son needs limits and respectful follow-through while he learns how to make good decisions on his own. Educate yourself about his school and his friends. Set reasonable limits and remain available to him.

- O **Recognize that your son's priorities are different than yours.** You may be concerned about curfew, grades, and household chores; your son is more likely to be concerned with the zit on his forehead and the girl who sits next to him in math.

- O **Accept that you cannot control your son.** You can guide, teach, support, and encourage your adolescent son; occasionally, you will have to follow through with an agreement. But you cannot control your son's thoughts, feelings, or actions. He must learn to do that himself.

- O **Let go when it is appropriate.** Your son needs room to practice adult skills and attitudes. He will certainly make mistakes, but he can learn a great deal from them if you allow him to. Parents who cling too tightly usually find that their son pushes them away.

Through all of this adolescent change, get to know the man your son is becoming. Change can be difficult for parents and for teens, but change is inevitable when you raise a son. He cannot remain your little boy, but he will welcome your presence in his life when it is offered with love and respect.

Setting Appropriate Limits

The day comes for every parent when they realize that they will not have their child forever—a few more years and he will be on his own. Every decision you make during these years has implications for the future.

You must recognize and acknowledge who you want this young man to become.

CHARACTER AND SKILLS

Imagine that you are teaching your son to drive. You may have begun by talking to him while you drive the car, pointing out the steering, braking, and rules of the road he will need to master. Eventually, your son takes the wheel while you sit in the passenger seat. He operates the car; you are there to offer guidance (and the occasional gasp of shock). At long last, the day arrives when your son drives off alone, while you stand in the driveway hoping you have taught him everything he needs to know.

A 2000 YMCA study found that not having enough time together with parents was the top concern among the 200 teenagers surveyed. Parents were far more concerned about drugs and alcohol. Spending time with their teenagers was the fourth most important priority for parents. Both parents and teens blamed parents' work obligations for not having enough time to spend together.

Life with a teenage boy is a great deal like teaching him to drive. You spend his early years teaching him, through words and action, the skills and attitudes he needs. As he grows, you make room for him to try things himself, with your support and supervision. Eventually he leaves home to live his own life, while you watch, hope, and love from a distance. If you try to steer his life for him, he may feel he has no choice but to eject you from his car. Conscious parents understand that their task is to teach their son, to support him as he learns, and eventually, to let go and allow him to live life on his own.

Fear sometimes causes parents to micromanage, overprotect, or rescue their teenage sons. But there is a better way. You can use the everyday issues of life with your son to teach him responsibility, problem-solving skills, and accountability.

MAKE AN AGREEMENT TOGETHER

Teenagers believe in respect—if they are treated respectfully. Many teens report that they feel disrespected by parents and teachers, which prompts them to be disrespectful in response. Teens are far more likely to cooperate with limits and rules that they have had a voice in creating and that they know in advance. The best way to set limits for teens is to include them in the process.

No matter how close you are to your son, chances are he is not likely to confide all the details of his life to you. Say, for example, your son comes to you and asks to go over to a friend's house with several other kids—including girls—for a movie night. You of course remember your own high school years and how intoxicating first romances can be. But you also love your son and are willing to risk his annoyance to ensure that he doesn't end up in a potentially dangerous situation. Before you give him permission to go on his night out, make an agreement together. Clearly write down the terms of the agreement. (Putting an agreement with your son in writing will make misunderstandings later far less likely.) For example:

1. Your son will give you the phone number of the host's house so that you can make contact with the parents. You agree that your son will be allowed to go as long as one parent is at home the entire time.

2. Your son must be home by 11:00. Your son may argue for a later time (with much eye-rolling and sighing), but remain firm. Perhaps you could agree, however, that if this evening goes well, you may consider a later curfew next time.

3. Your son cannot leave the host's house without calling you. If he goes anywhere else without letting you know, he will give up the privilege of going out for the next two weeks.

After you and your son sign the agreement, all that remains is following through. If your son follows the agreement he has made with you, he earns your trust and, perhaps, future privileges. If the agreement is broken, you can follow through without yelling or lecturing. When two weeks have passed, you can make a new agreement, and your son can try again.

As your son grows older and more mature, he will want more freedom. You can sit down with him in advance and respectfully make an agreement about what will happen and when. By allowing him to participate in the process, you teach him the skills of using good judgment and planning. By following through with dignity and respect, you teach trust and accountability.

You will not be able to prevent your son from making mistakes and poor choices, but you can make it possible for him to stay connected, accept your help, and learn from his mistakes. Listen well, remain calm, and use mistakes as opportunities to learn together.

Using Engaged Listening

Listening is one of the most important skills in your parenting toolbox. It is an important way to support your child and demonstrate that you care, and it can help you strengthen your relationship at any age. Listening is a tricky concept because it is not immediately obvious what you actually do when you listen. Engaged listening, otherwise known as active listening, is a process by which you give someone else your complete attention.

Engaged listening is particularly important when conversing with adolescents, who are much moodier and prone to withdrawal from parents. If your teen is telling you something, *anything*, it will go a long way to actively listen to whatever it is he is talking about. Don't give advice; don't talk about yourself (unless asked). Simply listen. Sometimes that is the best form of support you can possibly offer.

SETTING ASIDE DISTRACTIONS

All too often people multitask their way through the day. This is a coping mechanism you have probably developed as a means of juggling the many projects, tasks, errands, and obligations that you are responsible for. Although it is a common way to manage the multiple things you have to do, it splits your attention in a way that distracts your mind and actually lessens the quality of your attention. In reality, heavy multitasking causes your work and social interactions to suffer because of how it divides your focus.

There are times when your son wants to talk and tell you about something, but you have something else that needs to get done first. If you know you cannot give your child the attention he needs, communicate it to him: "Hey, my friend, I can't wait to talk to you and listen to your story. Before I can do that, though, I need to finish XYZ. How about you give me a hug and go play, and as soon as I'm finished you can tell me all about it. Sound good?"

To avoid this becoming an issue between you and your son (and to make sure you're modeling the kind of focus and engagement you want him to manifest in his own life), make sure to practice engaged listening when you are at home with your family. This means setting aside other distractions, making eye contact, and giving the speaker (in this case, your child) your full attention. There are many people who believe that they are strong and active listeners, when in reality this is not necessarily true. In fact, research suggests that people remember only 25–50 percent of what they hear.

WHERE IS YOUR MIND?

Even if you set down what you are doing and look at your son while he is talking, check in with yourself. Is your mind focused on what your child is saying, or is it still planning, scheduling, remembering, projecting, or worrying? It is very easy to only half-listen, and this can be especially true when it comes to listening to children.

The stories your child tells are not always relevant to your adult life. The idea behind active listening is not that you suddenly care about such and such problem his friend had in school today; it's that you care about your son, and he wants to tell you the funny, strange, or interesting things that he experienced that day.

It's true that you might not always find the topic interesting; the important part of this interaction is that your boy wants to share his joy, curiosity, and interests with you. He wants to interact with you, he wants to share parts of himself and his life with you, and this is one of the ways he can do that. Please don't miss out on this gift, even if the subject itself bores you. You'll be surprised by the interest you may develop in these things as you listen to your child talk about whatever. When a person you love cares about something, it becomes easier to see that "something" through their eyes and come to appreciate it all the more.

HOW TO PRACTICE ENGAGED LISTENING

Here is how to practice engaged or active listening and hone your listening skills during conversations:

○ **Remove distractions and tune in.** It's impossible to really listen to what someone is saying when there are distractions in the background. Turn off the television or radio, stop what you are doing, and make it clear to the other person that the conversation is your top priority.

○ **Pay attention to the person speaking.** Engaged listeners provide many clues that they are paying attention. Eye contact is important, and demonstrates to the person speaking that you are right there with him. Body language (such as leaning slightly toward the speaker) does the same thing. Verbal and nonverbal cues (such as nodding your head and saying "yes" or "mm-hmm") encourage the speaker to continue.

○ **Connect with the speaker.** Even if the content of the conversation is not initially interesting, remind yourself that you care about the person talking. Use that as your gateway to caring about the content. Think to yourself, *I care about you. What you're talking about is important to you, and I like that you are inviting me into your world.*

- **Ask clarifying and reflecting questions.** These are great ways to show that you are engaged with the subject matter. Repeat/reflect different points to make sure you understand ("So wait, if I'm hearing you right . . .") or, when appropriate, ask questions that expand the topic or invite different perspectives ("What do you think about . . .").

- **Listen; don't plan.** Oftentimes in conversations, people are simply waiting for their turn to talk. This is the opposite of listening. Although it is tempting to formulate responses in your mind, hold that impulse at bay until the other person is finished talking.

- **Be aware of your mind.** Thoughts have a tendency to wander, and are often sparked by the topic of conversation at hand. When you notice your mind wandering, gently turn your attention back to the speaker.

Engaged listening is another way to show how much you love and support your child by intentionally making him a priority, and how you model this skill will heavily influence how your child learns to communicate with family, friends, and teachers. When you practice engaged listening with your child, it demonstrates that you care about him, his opinions, his experiences, and his ideas. It indicates that you value him, because what he has to say is an extension of who he is and you recognize that he is trying to share that with you. In turn, you model for your child what it means to give someone your full attention. It's a powerful gift to you both that will keep you connected by putting your relationship first.

Teaching Life Lessons

The world seems to become a larger, scarier place when your son is a teenager. Most parents remember the moment their sixteen-year-old child grabbed the car keys for the first time, grinned, and walked out the door. Suddenly, you realize that you cannot control your son, protect him, or keep him out of trouble.

Rather than focusing on controlling your son's choices and behavior (which is impossible anyway), think carefully about what you want your son to think, feel, and decide about himself, you, and the world around him. Each time a new issue presents itself, you can use these life lessons as a guide in setting limits and making agreements.

Unfortunately, lectures and commands are usually ineffective with teenagers, who are highly skilled at using words to provoke power struggles. Rather than having yet another debate with your son, consider using actions rather than words. Nonverbal signals, such as looking at your watch or smiling without saying anything, are more effective with teens than long-winded lectures.

Your expectations and values will not be exactly the same as those of other parents. What matters is that you know your son well and have a good understanding of what he needs to learn to become a capable, responsible young adult. The following are some ideas about applying conscious parenting techniques to common issues that will arise with your teen son.

CURFEW

There is no right time for your son to be home. Sit down with him when both of you are calm and talk about his plans and your expectations. How old is your son? Is there a legal curfew for adolescents in your community? How well do you know his friends? Cell phones have made it simple for teens to disguise their actual location; like it or not, there is no way you can have absolute control of your son's whereabouts. Instead, let him know your concerns and agree together on a reasonable curfew. You should also decide in advance what will happen if he fails to come home on time. Be sure that you are willing to follow through before finalizing your agreement.

DRIVING

In most states, teenagers are allowed to have a learner's permit when they are fifteen and a half and can drive with an adult in the car. Some states, however, are considering raising the age at which a teen can get a driver's license. You should know the exact requirements in your own community. It is also wise to agree with your son about which car(s) he can drive; who will pay for insurance, gasoline, maintenance, and repairs; and what will happen if he gets a ticket. Will he be allowed to have friends in the car? To drive after dark? Put your agreement in writing and have your son sign it. You will need to refer to it more than once as he masters this important adult skill.

DATING

Most boys begin dating by going out with a group of friends, but at some point, your son is likely to want to spend time alone with one friend in particular. Again, it is impossible to control your son's preference in partners or his moment-to-moment behavior. Instead, talk with your son respectfully about your own values with regard to love, sex, and relationships. He may not agree with you, but it is important to share your own beliefs about dating. Do your best to keep your connection with your son strong and to remain approachable. Don't be surprised (and try not to take it personally) if your son prefers to discuss dating with Dad or another close male figure, rather than with Mom.

Power is extremely important to adolescents, who are actively working on the process of individuation. Teens and parents frequently find themselves engaged in power struggles in which parents insist while teens resist. If your son attempts to draw you into a power struggle, withdraw with dignity, follow through on your agreement, or take time to cool off before reacting.

SCHOOL

While many boys do well in high school and enjoy their studies, many more would rather be doing almost anything else than sitting in class or wrestling with homework. High school can become an arena for huge power struggles between a teen and his parents as decisions about the future loom on the horizon. It is helpful to know your son's school administrators and counselors and to be aware of his progress, but remember that school is your son's responsibility, not yours. Most teens resent parents who are overly intrusive or controlling; some even fail classes or refuse to do homework just to show parents that "you can't make me." It usually works best to sit down periodically with your son and talk calmly about his goals and his expectations for the future. Remember, too, that organizational skills are something that must be learned and practiced. Your son may appreciate your help in structuring his time so that work, school, and other tasks go smoothly.

Enjoying Your Son

It is certainly easy to get caught up in the struggles and worries of adolescence. You may look at your almost-adult son and hear a clock ticking insistently in the background. Time is running out, and there is so much for him to learn. Nevertheless, the boy you have always loved still lives within that changing body, despite the occasional bout of defiance and awkward moment.

You may feel anxious as your son experiments with new behavior and spends more time with his friends and less with you. Many adolescent boys require more privacy than ever before and may retreat into silence when unhappy or angry. You and your son may have difficult moments; he may lie, sneak out, or come home drunk. He may skip school or flunk important classes. He may dent your new car or have a party in your home when you're out of town. Even the most loving and responsible son will make mistakes, and some of them may be pretty shocking.

If you focus only on your son's negative behavior, the teen years will be unpleasant for both of you. Instead, concentrate on remaining a conscious parent and building a solid relationship. Here are some ideas:

- **Show curiosity.** Teens are often passionate about music, politics, or social issues. Invite your son to share his interests and beliefs; focus on listening rather than debating with him.

- **Be available.** You may be surprised how often your son flops down to talk with you if you're simply there. You may also consider making a regular lunch date or setting aside time to kick a ball around or share a hobby.

○ **Appreciate your son's positive qualities.** Even the most troubled teen has strengths; you just may have to look a bit harder to find them. Be sure your son knows what you like about him, as well as what you worry about.

There is much to love about your adolescent boy. Invest time in yourself and your adult relationships so that you can keep your perspective. Then do your best to relax, focus on teaching character and skills, and have fun whenever you can.

Important Points to Consider

Adolescence is a confusing and disorienting time in any child's life and it can cause many challenges for parents and kids alike. Being available to your son is one of the most important things you can do for him during this time. He may not always want to communicate with you, but knowing you are there for him if he does can go a long way. It's also important to remember to not take things too personally during these years. Your son is growing physically and emotionally and it can be unsettling for him. He is simultaneously searching for independence and afraid to find it. Be as compassionate and understanding as you can and remember that your son does still need some limits set for his own safety and well-being. Here are some points you should consider:

○ Adolescent boys need involved, active, conscious, and supportive parenting.

○ Brain development and hormones have a profound impact on the behavior of adolescent boys.

○ Taking time out to listen to and provide support for your son during his adolescent years will help him develop a stronger sense of self.

○ Your son's adolescent years will be filled with "teachable moments." Don't let those moments pass you by. Communicate your own life lessons to your son so he can learn from you.

 **CHAPTER 11**

Teaching Your Son Character

As your son approaches manhood, he will face many temptations. Before he can make decisions with confidence, he must have the belief that he is capable; he must know that his decisions matter and that he himself has worth. Character is who you are, not what you do. Many parents believe that if they love their children enough, give them what they want, and carefully control their behavior, their children will turn out to be good people. It doesn't always work out that way. *Character*—having an innate moral compass and the ability to think and act for oneself—does not come from being pampered or controlled, nor can it be given to children. Character must be taught.

Building Character

One important way of teaching your son that he is capable and competent is to teach him life skills. Even the simplest tasks of everyday life are opportunities for your son to learn that he can care for himself and for others, that he can make a meaningful contribution to the life of his family, and that he can influence the world around him.

When you watch a movie or a television program, invite your son to tell you how he would have reacted in a similar situation or what he thinks should have happened. Ask "what" and "how" questions and listen to his answers. Inviting him to think for himself and accepting his thoughts are important ways to teach values.

Teaching life skills may begin when your son is a toddler and you allow him to "help" you push the vacuum cleaner. As he gets taller and stronger, you can invite him to place napkins on the table, rinse lettuce for salads, or use a sponge to mop up spills. Notice that these tasks are not dreaded chores. They are opportunities to learn and to share the work of keeping a family running smoothly.

As your son grows, he can learn to cook nutritious meals, do his own laundry, mow the lawn, and change the oil in the car. Your attitude is key: If you approach these tasks as opportunities to teach skills and spend time working together, your son is less likely to be resistant. When the day comes that he leaves home, he will be able to take care of himself with confidence.

TEACHING CHARACTER BY MODELING

From the day your son was born, he has been watching you constantly for clues about how life should be lived. You may as well know from the beginning that the old saying "Do as I say and not as I do" will not work with your son. Like it or not, you are your son's most influential teacher, and your actions teach him his first lessons about character. He will be watching to see how you treat other people, how you behave in public places, and what things you value most.

Children are astonishingly perceptive, especially when it comes to adult hypocrisy. Your actions are a far more powerful teacher than your words; your son will assume that if you do it, so can he. Difficult as it may be, living your beliefs honestly is the best way to teach character.

You may fear that admitting mistakes or appearing less than perfect may damage your relationship with your son. In truth, when you can acknowledge your own errors and admit your failings, your son will be able (with time and practice) to do the same. The only way to teach character is to demonstrate it yourself.

Give Encouragement, Not Praise

Praise is everywhere. Parents pay children a dollar for each A on their report cards. Parents applaud every scribbled drawing as the best they've ever seen. Teachers hand out stickers, pencils, and pizza lunches for good behavior; smiley faces adorn acceptable homework papers.

Adults praise children for good reasons: They want to encourage appropriate behavior and they believe praise will build self-esteem. Unfortunately, praise is like junk food; a little bit may be acceptable, but too much can ruin your health.

THE PITFALLS OF PRAISE

Praise is usually offered when children succeed at tasks or live up to adult expectations. But what happens to the child who tries his best and always falls a little short? And what happens when children begin to need praise in order to feel valued?

A 1998 American Psychological Association study showed that children who are given constant praise begin to depend on it for their sense of self-worth. These children need to be admired, and when they encounter someone who does not like or admire them, the researchers found, they are more likely to become aggressive.

Praise can have unintended consequences. Too much praise does not build competence, a sense of capability, or character.

ENCOURAGEMENT

The word *encourage* comes from an Old French word meaning *to give heart to*. It is easy to praise children who behave well, earn awards, or excel at school, but what do you say to your son when he is discouraged, has misbehaved, or is having a difficult day? Praise would be insincere; it is encouragement he needs.

In their book *Encouraging Children to Learn*, Don Dinkmeyer, PhD, and Rudolf Dreikurs, MD, wrote, "Each child needs encouragement like a plant needs water." (In fact, so do all humans—parents included!) You can encourage your son by noticing the small things he does well, instead of waiting until he succeeds at the entire task. For instance, you might say, "You worked really hard at getting dressed this morning. Good for you!" You can offer this encouragement even though his pants are on backward, his shirt doesn't match, and his shoes are on the wrong feet. It is encouraging to say, "Wow! You got four Bs on your report card. You should feel proud of yourself." It is not encouraging to add, "And if you just try harder next time you could get As."

Offering encouragement can be difficult for family members who are used to pointing out problems and failings. Begin a family tradition of looking for the positive. Teach your children to compliment each other, say thank you, and notice what is right rather than only what is wrong. Looking for the positive encourages everyone in your family.

Encouragement says, "I see you trying and I appreciate you." Encouragement allows your son to feel valued and to have a sense of belonging even when he doesn't quite live up to your expectations. Encouragement builds connection—so vital to a boy's emotional health—and helps him learn from his mistakes and gather courage to try again. Encouragement also focuses on the person your son is becoming, rather than the things he can (or cannot) do. Offering loving encouragement is an important conscious parenting skill and an effective way to nurture your son's character.

Teaching Responsibility

It is an axiom of parenting that when parents take on too much responsibility children take on too little. After all, why should your son be responsible when you do everything so well? Responsibility—the ability to accept ownership of your mistakes and successes, to follow through with a task, and to do what you have promised—is one of the most important elements in good character. It is also one of the qualities that many parents fear their children will never learn.

RESPONSIBLE PARENT, IRRESPONSIBLE CHILD

You may help your son with his homework and pick up after him because you love him. But when you are responsible for all of his everyday needs, what is your boy learning? You undoubtedly want your son to become a responsible young man, one who is reliable, confident, and true to his word. Doing too much for him or failing to teach him accountability, however, is likely to encourage him to be irresponsible instead.

The truth is that the sort of conscious parenting that builds character and responsibility may not feel good to you. It is usually more fun to give your son what he wants (rather than what he needs), and it is undoubtedly more efficient to do household chores yourself rather than make room for your son to try. Your son will learn responsibility when you create opportunities for him to practice. Here are some suggestions:

- **Encourage your son to do whatever he can for himself.** Your son may not do tasks to your standards, but he will learn more by doing them himself than by watching you. If you wait on him hand and foot, he will expect you to continue.

- **Don't punish your son for making mistakes.** Teach him to accept them and learn from them. Kind, firm parenting and discipline designed to teach will allow your son to admit his mistakes without fear or shame.

○ **Allow your son to experience the results of his own choices.** It is tempting (and may feel more loving) to rescue your son when he gets into trouble, fails to do a task, or is lazy or uncooperative, but it rarely teaches responsibility and character.

○ **Follow through with agreements.** Your son will learn trust and accountability when you follow through. Be kind, firm, and respectful and do what you have agreed to do.

○ **Teach problem-solving skills.** A calm, friendly discussion is often the best way to help your son understand why things went awry and how he can get a different result next time. Teaching your son *how* to think is more valuable than teaching him *what* to think.

INVITE COOPERATION WITH FAMILY MEETINGS

Cooperation is the ability to work with others, contribute to a shared goal, and compromise when necessary. Rather than commanding, directing, and expecting, focus on inviting cooperation from your son. He is more likely to cooperate and contribute when you listen to his ideas, invite his suggestions, and work with him on making a plan to get things done.

One way of inviting cooperation is to have regular family meetings to offer encouragement and compliments, solve problems together, and enjoy family fun. (You can have successful family meetings when your son is as young as four.) Family meetings should not become gripe sessions. Begin each meeting with compliments for things done well during the week.

You can post an agenda board where anyone can list problems that need attention; then you can brainstorm together for possible solutions. It is usually better to work toward a consensus rather than take a vote. ("Losers" rarely enjoy family meetings.) You can finish your meeting with a snack, a movie, or a family activity. Working together to solve problems teaches children cooperation and allows them to feel a sense of belonging and significance.

Foster Compassion

Ask adults which gender is more likely to feel and express empathy, and most will tell you that girls are more empathic. In truth, boys have a tremendous capacity for empathy, kindness, and compassion; they begin life exquisitely tuned in to the feelings of others. Unfortunately, traditional cultural ideas about masculinity and appropriate male behavior sometimes lead boys to believe that demonstrating empathy and kindness is a form of weakness.

NURTURE A KIND SPIRIT

Boys desperately need the opportunity to learn gentleness and strength, conviction and compassion. The world is quick to teach our boys about toughness but offers few lessons in kindness. Consider making empathy and compassion part of your life together as a family. Here are some ideas:

- Talk openly with your son about social issues, bigotry, the environment, and war, keeping in mind his age and maturity level. Allow him to form his own opinions, but encourage the development of compassion and idealism.

- Talk about the feelings of others. When you watch television or the news, or are simply out in your community, you can talk with your son about how people may be feeling and what might be helpful to them.

- Act on your own ideas. Demonstrate generosity, kindness, and awareness of others when you are with your son. Actions do speak louder than words.

- Make caring part of your family life. You may adopt a needy family to purchase gifts for during the holidays, work together for an environmental cause, or get involved in a community project. Be sure empathy is a normal part of daily life in your home.

Remember, as your son enters the world of men, his peers and his culture will teach him what masculinity means. You will have the comfort of knowing that underneath his cool surface beats a kind and compassionate heart.

Encourage Integrity

A wise person once defined the word *integrity* as doing the right thing even when no one is watching. A number of recent studies have revealed that each succeeding generation values honesty a little less and is more likely to believe lying, cheating, and stealing are not only acceptable but also necessary to achieve success. These same studies have shown that boys are more likely than girls to be cynical about ethics.

The Josephson Institute of Ethics conducts regular studies on ethical behavior in teenagers and young adults. In 2008, they found that 64 percent of young adults had cheated on an exam, 42 percent had lied to save money, and 30 percent had stolen from a store. Some dismissed the results of this study, assuming that "kids will be kids" and ethical behavior would develop as they matured.

The 2009 Josephson Institute of Ethics study reveals some disturbing trends, however. Teenagers younger than seventeen are five times more likely than those older than forty to believe that lying and cheating are *necessary* to succeed, nearly four times as likely to deceive their bosses, and more than three times as likely to keep change given to them by mistake. There is a strong link between these beliefs in adolescence and later adult dishonesty; adults who admitted cheating on high school exams two times or more are more likely to be dishonest later in life.

If you want your son to become a person of integrity, you will have to consciously teach ethical behavior in the face of widespread dishonesty. It is not an easy task, but the future of our shared society may well depend on your success.

Spirituality in Your Son's Life

Numerous studies of healthy families have discovered a somewhat surprising fact: Families that appear to thrive, stay connected, and launch healthy children share something that can be called a spiritual life. It is important to note that spirituality is not the same thing as religion, nor does spirituality refer to any particular belief system. True spirituality means having a connection to something that is greater than one person and that provides a source of support during difficult times.

Recent studies show that eating dinner as a family is one of the most effective ways to prevent emotional and behavioral problems for children as they mature. Turn off the television, gather everyone around the table, and eat dinner together two or three times each week. Talk together about issues and ideas, building stronger connections for all of you.

As they grow, children usually have lots of questions about spiritual issues. They wonder what happens when people die or where babies wait to be born. They may feel anxious about their own mortality or angry that good people become ill or are hurt by others. Children, especially during the teen years, can be intensely idealistic; they talk frequently about what's fair or not fair. Any cause they adopt, whether it is political, social, or cultural, is likely to be pursued with their entire energy.

If a religious institution is part of your family's life, you already have a framework for discussing these issues with your son. Be aware that as your son grows older, he may question the principles or requirements of your faith. (Teens often choose issues important to parents as ways to express their individuation; for example, sons of atheistic parents sometimes become ardently religious.) Your spiritual life and ideas will become the foundation for your son's own inner life.

Simply caring about and connecting with a group, a community, or a cause can be a spiritual outlet, too. Your son's life will be richer (and his character is likely to be stronger) if you encourage him to thoughtfully consider some of the global issues we all face. Listen to your son's ideas (even if you don't agree with his positions) and encourage him to care.

Supporting Resilience and Self-Reliance

Resilience is the ability to cope with discouragement, failure, or setbacks and to be willing to try again. Resilience is an important characteristic of successful people, whether in business, sports, politics, or relationships, and most children are far more resilient than their parents think. You may know in your heart that protecting your son from hurt and disappointment is not really possible, but you may not realize that this sort of over-protection may actually cripple his ability to be resilient and discourage him from trying anything new.

Thomas Edison tried countless experiments before inventing a working light bulb. He said later that from each failure he learned something that eventually led to success. You can nurture resilience in your son by not exaggerating his failures (or rescuing him from them). Instead, talk together about what he might be able to learn for the future.

Like it or not, your son is destined to experience frustration, rejection, and even failure. Take time to understand and empathize with your son's feelings, but focus your energies on teaching him to cope with failure and disappointment. What might happen next time? What things can he do or say that will get a different result?

SELF-RELIANCE AND CHARACTER

Mark Twain once quipped that good judgment comes from experience, and experience comes from bad judgment. Both mistakes and successes are opportunities to learn, but surprisingly, many people learn more from their mistakes. Your goal is to teach your son how to be resilient and allow him to practice in an atmosphere of acceptance and respect; model empathy, integrity, and compassion for him; and allow him to grow his own sense of competence and capability. You may just discover that he becomes a self-reliant, confident person—a man of real character.

Supporting Social-Emotional Development

As your child progresses through adolescence you have less and less direct control over him as a parent. At this point your influence over him is directly proportional to the strength of your relationship, so you would be well advised to put the relationship first.

SET BOUNDARIES

Putting the relationship first does not mean letting your adolescent get away with anything he wants, or backing away from confrontations or disputes. On the contrary, it is all the more important that you share your voice, but you must learn to do so differently than you did when your child was younger. You are no longer in a position to dictate to your child, and instead must become comfortable and adept at engaging him in conversation and consideration.

Whatever boundaries or rules you have put in place with your young adult, it is imperative to follow through on the agreed-upon consequences. Not following through on consequences to problematic behavior undermines your position as parent, and teaches your teen that he can do whatever he wants.

BE MINDFUL

One of the greatest challenges of parenting adolescents is backing off and letting them take more responsibility for their own lives and solving their own problems. This can be stressful for parents, as it often puts you in the position of having to watch your child suffer.

It is very easy for parents of teens to worry about the future. Therefore, it can be helpful to have a way of directly attending to your own concerns and fears about your adolescent before engaging with him. Here is a technique that can help:

1. Begin by identifying a worry or concern you have about your teenager.

2. Think about what you have seen that gave rise to this worry. What was it that got your attention? Why do you take this as cause for concern? Be particularly sensitive to any associations you may make between what is happening for your teen and things that happened in your own life. It is very easy for parents to relive challenges they faced in their own lives when similar things come up for their children.

3. Try to identify specifically what you think will happen to your child. What are you afraid of?

4. Now sit with these thoughts and sensations for a while, breathing deliberately with them. Try to recognize them as just stories. You are not trying to dismiss them, just to put them in the proper context. When you are ready, take a few deep breaths and move on.

The purpose of this practice is not to let go of any thoughts or fears you may have, but rather to contextualize them more appropriately so that you can be there for your child as he needs you. When you are gripped by your own fears for your child and the stories you tell based on those fears, any attempt to engage your teen will be colored by that emotional cloud. What you say to your teenager will be driven by these fears, and you will act in a way that focuses on your own concerns instead of attending to what he is dealing with. This practice can help you to be more available to your teen through almost any circumstance.

BE AN ACTIVE LISTENER

It can be difficult for parents to really listen to their adolescent children. Often, when you engage your adolescent, you can be completely overwhelmed. Adolescents regularly talk very fast and with great intensity. It can be hard to keep up with all the people involved and their relationships, let alone the slang and other language your teen may use. If you attempt to offer solutions to your teen's problems, you may be left dumbfounded when his frustration boils over and he lashes out at you. To really be there for your adolescent you need to practice active listening with him, and then separately deal with anything that may come up in your own mind as you do so.

Part of being a conscious parent is giving your teen your full attention when you are listening to him. Stop doing anything else and use your body language to help create a safe space for him to share. As he begins to talk, listen intently to what he says as he speaks, and notice the way that he expresses himself. You may not be able to follow the cast of characters involved, and may also have trouble keeping up with exactly what happened, but these are just details. Remember that the most important piece of this interaction is your presence.

By listening intently you give your teen an opportunity to vent some of his emotions and process events for himself. Do not interrupt him; just try to let him talk. Resist the temptation to offer advice unless he explicitly asks for it. The purpose of this exercise is to be a sounding board for him, letting him express his feelings about a situation and explore it in his own mind. He will figure out for himself what he needs to do about it, and this may include asking for your help, but it very well may not. Either way, you can support him with your presence as he sorts things out.

Important Points to Consider

Character can indeed be taught. The ability to choose correctly and ethically can be formed by teaching your son responsibility and life skills and by modeling character yourself. It certainly isn't always an easy or comfortable process, but building character in your son is one of the greatest gifts you can offer him. Here are some important points to consider when raising your son:

○ Modeling is one of the most valuable teaching tools for boys and girls alike. Your son will learn about character by watching you demonstrate your own, so remember in all your daily interactions to model the traits you want your son to learn.

○ There is a difference between encouragement and praise. Encouragement expresses your appreciation for your son's efforts whether or not he succeeds in his attempts, which can have a powerful effect on the man he becomes.

O Encourage your son to try things on his own and to follow through with his commitments. If you wish your son to learn to take responsibility for his actions, you must give him the opportunities to do things for himself.

 **CHAPTER 12**

Dealing with Risky Behavior

Like it or not drug and alcohol use and other risk-taking behaviors are prominent in modern society, and at some point your son will likely be exposed to them. What are you as a conscious parent supposed to do? You can't actually control your son's choices when it comes to risky behavior, but you can definitely inform those choices with the best information and understanding you have. You can educate your son about the nature of the problem, about the risks involved, and about keeping safe.

The Lure of Vice

Because teens do not yet have fully developed prefrontal cortexes and are not able to control impulses as well as adults, they are more likely to take risks on the spur of the moment or because their friends do. And because adolescent brains are wired to learn new habits and patterns quickly, teens have a higher risk of addiction than do adults. They also have a strong need to belong with the group and an inherent desire to show adults that "you can't make me." All of this makes drinking and drug use extremely attractive.

Many teens (and many boys) drink for the same underlying reasons their parents do: They feel stressed or anxious (being a teenager isn't always easy), and drinking helps them relax. Alcohol and drugs are also part of a teen's social scene; parties often include booze, pot, and other substances.

According to Dan Kindlon, PhD, and Michael Thompson, PhD, almost four out of every ten male high school seniors have smoked pot. Two-thirds of all male high school seniors have been drunk; 7 percent smoke pot every day. Boys are also more likely than girls to try "harder" drugs such as cocaine, heroin, ecstasy, and LSD.

Unfortunately, alcohol does not improve judgment and problem-solving abilities, and the potential for injury or serious trouble goes up when boys drink. Some statistics show that in countries where the legal drinking age is lower, teens find drinking less attractive and do less of it. But in the United States, where alcohol is forbidden until the age of twenty-one, alcohol is a way of having fun and dealing with difficult emotions while demonstrating independence from parents.

THE RITES OF MALE BONDING

Sadly, boys often view attaining the ability to "hold your liquor" as a rite of passage into manhood. Cool guys drink and party, while nerds and geeks do not. A boy's natural urge to explore and experiment can be misdirected toward binge drinking and drug use when friends encourage it, and hangover stories—vomiting, crawling, or passing out—seem funny and admirable. "Man, I was so wasted!" or "I can't believe I did that!" are common expressions after a night of partying.

Boys often enjoy the feeling of invincibility that comes from an alcohol-induced buzz. They want to connect with their friends (and with girls) and find it simpler to do so when they are drinking together. It is often easier for a boy to talk honestly about his fears and feelings when he is drunk—and then to forget about it when he has sobered up.

Many parents fear drug and alcohol abuse more than any other risk factor in their sons' adolescence. And indeed, the dangers are real: Teens are killed while driving drunk, they overdose, or they have unprotected sex while under the influence of alcohol or drugs. They may also find themselves in trouble with the police for purchasing or possessing an illegal substance, causing trouble for themselves and their families.

Like it or not, most boys will try cigarettes, alcohol, and marijuana at some time during their adolescence. Adolescents believe they are immortal and rarely worry about the risks inherent in drinking. Experimentation and occasional use do not mean that a boy will develop a real substance abuse problem, but they are reasons for parents to be aware and concerned.

Be a Role Model

You have already learned that, much as you might wish to, you cannot control your son. You can only control yourself and what you teach him about practicing good judgment and self-discipline. You may worry about drinking and drug use because you experimented when you were younger, and you want to spare your son the problems you experienced. Or you may not like his friends and may worry about their influence on him. No matter how good your intentions, however, attempts to restrict your son's whereabouts, friends, or activities are likely to result in power struggles and conflict.

Pay attention to the aspects of your relationship with your boy that you *can* control. For instance, be aware of how much (and how often) you drink—and why. You are your son's most important role model; if you drink to relax or because you are stressed, you are teaching him that alcohol is an acceptable solution to his problems. If there is a history of alcohol or drug abuse in your family, it can be helpful to share that information with your son and to let him know that he may be at risk. (Some experts believe that genes play an important role in how we metabolize and react to alcohol.)

A Yale University study in 2000 found that the risk for substance abuse may be higher in affluent communities. Boys sometimes feel such pressure from parents to achieve and to be admitted to good colleges that they resort to substance use to relieve anxiety. In many affluent neighborhoods, boys who smoke or drink are among the most popular in their peer groups.

Be aware of your expectations for your son. Do you ask too much of him? How does he react to criticism, high standards, and parental disappointment? Remember that long silences, withdrawal from you, or unexplained changes in behavior may indicate trouble. Focus on your relationship. How strong is the connection between you?

Communicate Openly with Your Son

Too many parents spend a son's entire youth avoiding the subject of risky behavior. "Why bring it up?" they say. "I don't want to give him ideas. Anyway, he's never been in trouble." Hiding from the problem won't make it go away, however. If your son hasn't tried alcohol or marijuana, he undoubtedly has friends who have—and who will offer it to him.

KNOW WHERE YOU STAND

Knowing how to approach your son about drinking and drug use can be difficult, but it is essential that you do so. Your son may be embarrassed or angry; he may believe you're accusing him of bad behavior. But the benefits far outweigh the risks.

Start by talking about substance use early. You can talk with your son about drinking, smoking pot and cigarettes, or doing drugs as soon as he is old enough to know what they are. It is not helpful to alarm or frighten your son; simply let him know how you feel about drugs and alcohol. Be clear and consistent from the beginning. He may not always admit it, but your son cares about what you think.

Also be sure to let your son know that if he breaks the law, you will not rescue him. It is illegal for teens to purchase, possess, or consume alcohol or drugs. While marijuana laws are changing, in most communities it remains illegal for teens to smoke, possess, or sell pot. Be sure your son knows that if he chooses to break the law, he will be responsible for the consequences. You can support and love him without rescuing him.

GET TO KNOW HIS OUTLOOK

Conscious parenting involves devoting energy to being aware and informed. Make every effort to know your son's friends and their families— not to spy, but simply to create a caring community for all your children. It is also helpful to maintain open communication with his school and other groups. Much teen partying happens right after school, when parents are at work and houses are empty.

Encourage emotional awareness and expression. If your boy can talk about his feelings, fears, and needs, he may be less tempted to mask them with drugs and alcohol. You can't make your son talk, but you can certainly offer to listen.

Pay careful attention to your son's behavior, and get to know your son's ideas and opinions. Do you know what your son believes about drinking and drug use? What does he see going on around him? If you remain calm, don't lecture, and make yourself available, you may be surprised at how willing your son is to talk with you about drugs and alcohol.

Keep in mind that if you suspect that your son has a problem with alcohol or drug addiction, you should not hesitate to find professional help for him and for your family. You may be unpopular for the moment, but you may also save your boy's life.

DRINKING, DRUGS, AND DRIVING

Every year, far too many young people die or are seriously injured in alcohol- and drug-related automobile accidents. While having a beer in the backyard with friends may not be appropriate (it is illegal for teens, after all), the risks are far greater when teens party and then get behind the wheel—or get into a car with someone else who has been drinking.

As a parent, you can exercise some control over when your son drives. Discussions about his driving privileges may be a perfect opportunity to address the issue of drinking and drug use.

Consider making a written agreement with your son. Before your son begins driving on his own, sit down together and talk honestly about partying and driving. Be sure your son understands that it is never acceptable to drive when he has had a drink or used drugs. You may decide that if he violates the agreement, he gives up his right to drive for an agreed-upon period of time. Put your agreement in writing and sign it together, and then be willing to follow through if necessary.

Talk about what your son should do if he is without a safe ride. Make it clear that if he is faced with riding with someone who becomes drunk, he should *always* call you. Tell him that there will be no questions or lectures. His safety is most important—even if he is somewhere he's not supposed to be. (Be sure you can follow through with respect and dignity.) You will need to repeat this discussion throughout your son's adolescence.

You cannot afford *not* to have this discussion; neither can your son. Privately, you may believe that the law is too harsh or that a little partying won't really hurt your son, but keep in mind that the risks to your boy are serious and quite real. Talk openly and often with him about drugs and alcohol, driving, and partying.

Discussing Your Past

If you're raising a boy these days, chances are good that you, too, grew up in an era when drugs and alcohol were readily available. Many parents have their own memories of parties, sneaking past parents, and occasionally, some serious problems. You may believe that having a strong, open relationship with your son is important, but what if he expects that relationship to go both ways? You must think about what to do if your boy asks you about your own past behavior.

Even the best parent can fall prey to the fear of looking less than perfect in a son's eyes. Boys want to love and respect their parents, and parents want to be admired and respected. It can be difficult to find that you have fallen off your pedestal, but telling your own truth and honestly accepting it may be a powerful way of reaching out to your son.

Rather than glamorizing your own past exploits, take time to consider the lessons you want your son to learn. What do you want him to believe and decide about drinking and partying? If he asks (and most boys eventually do), you can share with him your own experiences, what you felt and thought, and most important, what you learned—or failed to learn. Remember, real discipline is teaching; sometimes an honest conversation can be the most effective discipline of all. Being real with your son may actually strengthen your connection.

Paying Attention Rather Than Spying

As a parent, worry and fear can become constant companions. When it's late at night, the house is quiet, and you're not absolutely sure where your son is, you may be tempted to wander into his room and search for clues. But what happens if you find what you're looking for?

THE FRAGILE BOND

Most boys (especially teenagers) consider their rooms to be private spaces. They are fiercely protective of their privacy and can become extremely angry when an anxious parent dares to open drawers or sift through a backpack. Parents sometimes believe that their desire to protect their son gives them the right to read journals, text messages, and e-mail; rummage through closets; eavesdrop on conversations; and even install hidden cameras. But boys rarely agree.

It takes years of work to build trust between a parent and a child, years of listening, sharing, and solving problems together. It is all too easy to damage that trust, and it is not always children who cause the damage.

Finding the marijuana your son has stashed under his socks may keep him from hiding it there again, but it is unlikely to improve either your relationship or his behavior. It is better to be alert and awake when your son comes home and to let him know you're paying attention.

Yes, you should be aware of your son's activities. It is entirely possible that there would be fewer school shootings and less juvenile crime if more parents were paying attention. Still, the best answer is to begin to build a relationship of trust and mutual respect in your boy's earliest years. Real connection often makes it possible to simply ask a boy what he is up to. Boys are surprisingly willing to tell the truth and even to ask for help with everything from drinking to stolen money when they believe their parents are willing to listen and work with them to solve problems.

IF YOU SUSPECT TROUBLE

If you know your son well, you will know when there is reason to worry. Unexplained absences from school, missing possessions or money, irrational behavior, or drastic changes in sleep or eating habits can be warning signals. It's usually wise to approach your son directly, calmly, and respectfully, and to let him know you're concerned about his safety and welfare—and that you want to help, not bust him.

If your son refuses to talk to you, however, you may decide you have no choice but to search his private possessions. If you find something troubling, talk to your son directly and tell him what you have done and why. Then focus on finding solutions, whatever that may mean. Be sure the message of love and concern gets through to your son.

Without good reason to spy, it's usually better to honor your son's privacy in the same way you expect him to honor yours. If you focus on listening, understanding, and truly connecting, you just may find that snooping is never necessary.

Boys and Smoking

Compared to the dangers of alcohol, marijuana, and other drugs, cigarettes may seem innocent, even benign. Yet the statistics are staggering; cigarettes, smokeless tobacco, and other trendy products, such as clove cigarettes, cause nicotine dependence, illness, and serious long-term health risks. Boys begin smoking for a variety of reasons. They may believe it looks cool or macho; after all, many celebrities smoke or chew.

Tobacco is undoubtedly the easiest substance for boys to acquire. About 25 percent of high school students smoke; boys who steal cigarettes from parents or borrow chew from friends or older siblings are usually happy to share.

According to a 2009 report by CNN and the Mayo Clinic, nicotine is as addictive to some people as heroin. It enhances the release of brain chemicals that are associated with pleasure, relaxation, and appetite suppression. Adolescent boys who begin smoking regularly typically show symptoms of nicotine dependence within 180 days of their first use. Two-thirds of teen smokers have made at least one unsuccessful attempt to quit.

Smoking may also allow an awkward, gangly teen to feel more mature and manly. Tobacco companies sometimes sponsor rodeos and auto races, making smoking seem normal and acceptable. And many parents smoke; in fact, boys whose mothers and fathers smoke cigarettes are far more likely to begin smoking themselves than boys with nonsmoking parents.

Smoking is not cool or harmless. Nicotine is highly addictive, and some experts estimate that as many as one out of three smokers will die of a tobacco-related illness. People who begin smoking before the age of sixteen are more likely to become lifelong smokers. There also appears to be a link between smoking, academic problems, and the eventual use of alcohol and other drugs.

You cannot keep your son from smoking or chewing if he decides to try, but you can influence your son's decision about smoking. Here's how:

○ **Talk to your son about tobacco.** As with so many other issues in raising your son, sharing information about the dangers of smoking is important. Make it clear to your son that you do not want him to smoke.

○ **If you smoke, consider quitting.** Your actions will send a more powerful message to your son than words alone.

○ **Limit access to tobacco.** If you choose to continue smoking, do not give cigarettes to your son or leave them where he can easily find them. Do not smoke in your house or allow your son to do so.

○ **Show your son how smoking affects him now.** Lectures about cancer, illness, and death have little effect on teens—they're immortal, remember? Instead, you can point out the amount of money cigarettes cost (and what he could buy instead), the smell, the coughing, and the effect on girls.

Samuel Johnson once said, "The chains of habit are too weak to be felt until they are too strong to be broken." Your son will inevitably be exposed to smoking, drinking, and alcohol as he makes his way through middle and high school, but you can help him make wise choices. Do your best to set a good example; talk to him often about the risks he faces. Above all, spend time together. When your son knows he belongs and has worth in his family, he is less likely to go looking for it elsewhere.

Important Points to Consider

Risky behavior is prominent in our world, and there is no way to shelter your son from it. But you can be open with him, communicate your feelings on the matter, and set yourself up as a role model for how to handle these situations. Here are some points to consider:

- Many young boys turn to risky behavior for the same underlying reasons that adults do (for escape or self-medication). However, because their brains are not fully formed yet, teens are more likely to become addicted and overindulge in risky behaviors.

- Though you cannot control your son, you can influence him through modeling and support.

- Open conversation, including communication about your own past, can help to address problem behaviors. Don't be afraid to be honest with your son about your past mistakes or regrets. He will appreciate your honesty and trust and may be able to learn from your experiences.

- Privacy is important to most boys, a fact to consider when determining how to communicate with him. While spying on your son may seem like the easy thing to do, it will create a rupture of trust you may not be able to heal.

 **CHAPTER 13**

Handling Sexuality

As puberty begins, limbs stretch, muscles thicken, the voice deepens, and new hair appears. Young men begin to experience all the pressures, desires, and anxieties that grown men feel. Most boys crave sexual experience. They may long for it and be terrified of it at the same time. Boys want to appear sophisticated and manly in front of their friends, but they also want genuine love and connection. It can be a hard balance to find for even the most mature young man. Be sure you stay connected to your son during these complicated years and that he has the information he needs to make wise, safe decisions.

Emerging Sexuality

Boys often have far more questions about puberty and sexuality than they are willing to express. For many boys, there is a glaring discrepancy between what they have always been taught about girls and women and what their peers and the culture push them to believe about sex. Your son may respect and admire his mother and love his sisters (well, most of the time), but he also feels increasing pressure to prove his manhood—and having sex seems to be the way to become a real man.

Like it or not, many teens (both boys and girls) become sexually active early in adolescence. Teens tend to adopt the culture of their peers and may have very different attitudes toward sex than their parents. They often have multiple partners and see sex as both a rite of passage and an entertaining social activity rather than a lifelong commitment. In the world of today's teens, love and sex do not necessarily go together.

An old saying with an element of truth states that girls use sex to get love and affection, while boys use love and affection to get sex. The pressure to prove himself sexually may lead even the nicest boy to treat girls in a cavalier manner. Teach your son that his desires are normal, but respect and kindness are essential.

Talk to Your Son about Sex

You should know from the beginning that if you don't teach your son about his body, sex, and sexuality, his friends will be more than happy to take your place—and far less likely to know what they're talking about. Sex involves far more than a physical act; it is an expression of emotions and intimacy, character and moral values. Your son will be curious about his body and how it works from his earliest years.

JUST THE FACTS, SON

Sex is everywhere in advertising and popular culture. It is used to sell everything from beer to automobiles, and even prime-time television is loaded with sexual innuendo. Nevertheless, Americans (including parents) can be surprisingly squeamish about sex. It is far easier to educate your son about his body and his sexuality when you are comfortable with your own.

It is best to use accurate terms to describe body parts and functions and to remain calm and relaxed while doing so. Your son needs to know that sex is normal and healthy; identifying body parts clearly and calmly will help. While baby talk is acceptable when he is a toddler, it is best to use terms such as *penis* or *breast* as he gets older.

It often surprises parents to learn that as many as one in four boys is sexually molested. Teach your son that he controls who touches his body and how. Only parents or a doctor (with a parent present) should be allowed to touch his private parts; he should feel confident about saying no and telling a parent if he feels uncomfortable.

Children are usually old enough to know about sex when they are old enough to begin asking. Offer simple answers to your son's questions without embarrassment. For example, if your son points to a woman's breasts and asks what those are, you can tell him women have breasts to feed babies. You might even show him a picture of himself nursing so he can understand. Remember, your son does not need all the excruciating details about sex just yet. Keep it simple; you can add information as he matures.

BEGIN THE CONVERSATION

You may remember the day your mother or father sat down with you to have "the talk," but those days are long gone. Because sex is so widely present in modern life, it usually works best to begin talking about sexuality with your son early. Puberty begins for most boys as soon as ten or eleven, when hormones begin changing both the brain and the body. Keep in mind that boys may feel a great deal of pressure to know everything about sex (or at least, more than their female partners).

Curiosity about sex is normal. Most boys acquire a copy of *Playboy* or the *Sports Illustrated* swimsuit issue sometime during early adolescence. Masturbation and nocturnal emissions (sometimes called "wet dreams") are also normal as boys mature, but they may hesitate to talk with you about these events. It may ease the process if you begin the conversation yourself. For instance, as your boy enters adolescence, you can let him know about the changes and urges he may experience. (Even moms can have these discussions. Your son may feel a bit embarrassed, but he will be grateful for the information.)

It is important that you talk early and often with your son about relationships. Dad, this especially means you: Male role modeling about respect, kindness, and real partnership is essential if your son is to grow up into a man who can enjoy the give-and-take of both sexual pleasure and caring relationships. Be sure that your own attitudes toward women and sex are those your son can emulate, and that your words and behavior toward his mom are respectful—even if you are no longer together.

Be Realistic and Available

Most schools these days offer detailed sex education programs. Your son will learn something about anatomy, what a condom is, and all about various sexually transmitted diseases. Unfortunately, most teens fail to apply what they learn in class to sex in the real world. Your son cannot have too much information about sexual health and safety, and you are still his best teacher.

Give some serious thought to what you want your son to learn about sex and how best to protect him. Before you even begin talking to your son, make sure that you are available and unshockable. Your attitude toward sex is important. If your son learns that you are willing to talk with him and that you are relaxed and approachable, he is more likely to come to you with his questions. Let your son know that you will always want to help him, even if he has made a mistake.

When talking to your son about sex, you must also discuss alcohol and drugs. Many teens have sex when they are drunk or high and are unprepared for the consequences. Be sure your son understands that partying may affect his ability to make good decisions.

To prepare for a discussion with your son about sex, it is best that you understand the anatomy of sex. Many boys enter puberty and experience sexual urges without ever having been taught what to expect. Accurate information about anatomy and function will be extremely helpful to your son. (If you just can't bring yourself to talk about it, ask a trusted male relative or check out one of the many excellent books or websites available. Let your son know he can ask you questions later.)

As teens get older, they become less willing to talk about sex with parents. One study found that more than half of fifteen-year-olds report that they rarely or never talk to their parents about sex, while twelve- and thirteen-year-olds talk with parents about sex more frequently. Begin talking with your son about sex while he is young—and still listening.

You absolutely must talk to your son about pregnancy and birth control. Most boys know very little about female anatomy, and many believe that girls can't get pregnant the first time they have sex. Be sure your son understands that condoms do not provide adequate birth control on their own. If he is not mature enough to discuss birth control with a partner, he is not mature enough to have sex.

Even if you believe your son may disagree with your views, share your morals and values with him. If you believe that sex belongs only in marriage, be sure to teach that belief to your son from the very beginning. You should also be willing to talk with your son about oral sex and other sexual activities, which are increasingly common among teens (and often not viewed as "real sex"). Be realistic, however. Even boys with solid values may choose to have sex before marriage, and many are afraid to tell parents when problems arise. Morals and sex education are not mutually exclusive; be sure your son has both.

Becoming Sexually Active

Your head may be spinning by now, especially if your son has not yet entered puberty. You might prefer that he not even think about sex until he has graduated from college, but you're unlikely to get your wish. Most boys experiment with some form of sexual activity, from making out to intercourse, long before they graduate from high school.

FROM PLAYMATE TO PARTNER

When boys are young, girls are nothing more than playmates. When boys reach the age of five or six, they usually realize that girls are different and begin to prefer their own gender for play and other activities. As puberty approaches, however, things begin to change. Some boys are interested in girls while still in elementary school, and others do not appear to care until quite a bit later. There's no "normal" age.

Inevitably, though, most boys figure out that sexual activity feels good and that girls may be part of the process. (Interestingly, many boys have close female friends throughout childhood and adolescence and can easily separate love from friendship.) Parents are often caught unaware when sons begin to show interest in girls in that way.

It may be helpful to check in with your son from time to time to see where he is in the process. It is also wise to think about when you will feel comfortable with your son dating, kissing, holding hands, and engaging in other related activities, and to talk openly with your son about "making out."

> Never minimize your son's feelings about a relationship—or a breakup. He may not be an adult, but his feelings are genuine and deserve your respect. If your son talks to you about his relationships, encourage him to trust his feelings, be honest and respectful, and make decisions he can live with.

YOUR ROLE IN YOUR SON'S SEXUALITY

As your son matures and begins to form new relationships, your role in his life will change. Mothers in particular can struggle with a son's growing independence and desire for privacy. While some boys bring their girlfriends home, others prefer to keep their personal relationships quite private. This does not mean they are doing something forbidden.

It is also best to refrain from pressuring your son about girls. You can be interested and aware, but allow your son space to find his own way. If he is not interested in dating, don't push him. If your son appears a bit too interested, you may need to work together to set reasonable limits. Take time to meet his girlfriends (and their parents) if you can; it simply makes life easier for all of you. Encouraging your son to entertain his friends at home may allow you to feel comfortable with his behavior.

Connecting with Your Gay Son

Although society may be more tolerant now than ever before, LGBTQ individuals still face an uphill battle in feeling accepted and in having the same rights to love, family, and privileges as heterosexuals do. According to William Pollack, PhD, between 5 and 10 percent of all men (from all religious, racial, and ethnic backgrounds) will recognize during adolescence or early adulthood that they are homosexual.

Despite the strongly held beliefs of some groups, available research tells us that boys do not choose to be homosexual any more than they choose to be straight. Sexual preference appears to be the result of a complex process, including the sexual hormones that bathe the fetus's brain.

Many boys (and girls) experiment with same-sex relationships and bisexuality as they grow up; only time will tell a boy's true sexual orientation. Curiosity about sex, gender, and relationships is a normal part of growing up. You cannot choose your son's sexual preferences. Be patient while he discovers his own sexual identity and accept him for who he is.

Many boys who are homosexual suffer depression, shame, and a sense of isolation from peers. Numerous studies show that gay teens are at an increased risk for substance abuse and depression; nearly one-third of gay teens have attempted suicide. Your acceptance and support are crucial to your son's health and well-being. If your son is gay, educate yourself, deal honestly with your own feelings, and stay connected.

You may have strong feelings about homosexuality; you may be shocked that your son is gay. You may even blame yourself. However, parenting appears to have very little to do with sexual preference. Studies of identical twins and other research appear to indicate that boys become homosexual because they are simply intended to; dominant mothers, absent fathers, and parenting style are not factors.

Not surprisingly, gay boys and teens need a sense of belonging and significance just as much as straight boys do. In fact, they usually have an even stronger need for acceptance and unconditional love from parents. Most parents of a gay son find that before they can wholeheartedly accept their son, they must deal with their own emotions and beliefs about homosexuality.

It is wise to recognize that homosexuality has very little to do with traditional notions of masculinity. Gay teens are just as able to be talented athletes as straight teens. They have a wide variety of interests and abilities. A gay boy must make decisions about himself and the world and develop his own preferences and strengths, just as any other boy must do. He needs your love and support.

If your son is gay and you are having trouble accepting this, it may be helpful to look for resources in your community. There are support groups for gay teens and their families; such groups can help you and your son feel comfortable and secure. If you or your son suspects that he is gay, it may also be helpful to find a skilled therapist to help you adjust, learn, and support each other.

Affection with Your Growing Son

As your son matures, you will likely find yourself adjusting to new boundaries of personal space and touching. Mothers often have some adjustments to make as their sons reach physical and emotional maturity. More than one mom has encountered her son coming out of the shower and been surprised at how much has changed. Fathers, too, must adjust to a son's approaching manhood, but the adjustment is often a bit easier, since they experienced it themselves.

Both parents, mothers and fathers, must learn to set new physical boundaries with growing sons. Chances are good that as he grows, your son will still love to have his back scratched, and hugs remain a wonderful way of expressing love and affection. However, many boys find that they want a bit more personal space than their parents are used to giving them.

Many mothers notice that their sons display rude and unpleasant behavior as they enter adolescence. Boys who are just becoming aware of sexuality may need to distance themselves from too much closeness with Mom. The more comfortable a boy becomes with his own sexuality, the more likely he is to once again demonstrate affection and connection with his mother.

If your son squirms away from hugs, kisses, or other physical contact, don't take it personally. It takes time for a boy to adjust to his own changing body, his new desires and feelings, and other changes in his physical landscape. Many boys find that the close physical relationship they once enjoyed with their mothers now feels uncomfortable. Mom is, after all, a girl.

Be conscious of the process your son is undergoing and give him time and space to feel comfortable as a young adult. It often works best to let him set physical boundaries and initiate touch, although you can certainly ask, "How about a hug?" As your son grows up, you will learn to transform your relationship into one between adults and equals. With your encouragement and understanding, your son will learn to have healthy and loving relationships of his own.

Important Points to Consider

The transformation into a sexual being can be a difficult period for both boys and parents. This period of healthy transition can be awkward and prove to be one of the most difficult times for parent and child to remain close and connected. Here are some considerations:

O Every boy matures at a different rate.

O You should discuss sexuality with your son at age-appropriate levels throughout his life. If you don't, he may be unprepared for and embarrassed about the changes in his body when he enters puberty.

O Your attitudes and relationships will have a profound impact on your son's view on sex. As in almost every area of parenting, being a role model is one of the best things you can do for your son. If he sees that you are open to discussing sexuality honestly he will tend toward this as well.

O If your son is gay it is important that you be accepting and understanding of him. Gay teens often have additional stress and challenges, and your son needs to know you love him for who he is.

O Continued communication and support are vital for your son's development into adulthood. Your physical relationship with your son may change, and he may wish for fewer outward signs of affection, but your son still needs to feel and know your love for him.

 **CHAPTER 14**

Encouraging Responsibility in Your Son

Every family defines what constitutes responsible behavior differently, depending on the values the parents hold. However, it is taught the same way in every family—by example and instruction. Your son will need the skills and confidence to support himself, make decisions, and thrive on his own. You must equip your growing son to find success and happiness as an independent adult. Raising a boy is a long-term process; the ultimate goal is to guide him toward a rewarding, happy, and productive adulthood.

Teach the Needed Skills

It is tempting (and often easier) to do tasks for your son. After all, little boys tend to leave a trail of messes behind them, and busy parents usually find it more expedient to do things themselves. But what happens when you're no longer around to cook the meals, provide the money, and find the missing baseball glove? Unless you plan on inviting your son to live in his bedroom indefinitely, he will need to learn how to handle adult responsibilities.

BEGIN EARLY

You may remember that self-esteem—a sense of one's worth and ability—grows out of skills and competency. Your son will not magically learn to fend for himself on the day he graduates from high school; his education in responsibility should begin with his first steps. No, he won't be capable of doing much when he is tiny, but you can begin to teach him valuable skills in small lessons. The wonderful part of this process is that when he is young, your boy will think helping you is fun!

> Involving your son in household tasks is not mean or demanding. Your attitude is important: If you believe that you are teaching your son valuable skills, he is more likely to believe it, too. You are demonstrating love and commitment when you teach him to do things himself and give him age-appropriate responsibilities.

Working and learning together also provide a way to talk, share, and connect. Here are some possibilities for teaching skills while your son is a child:

○ When he is two or three: he can undress himself, feed himself, take off shoes and socks, rinse vegetables, pick up toys, put napkins and silverware on the table, and put clothes in the hamper.

○ When he is four: he can brush his teeth, choose his own clothes, dress himself, put on shoes, measure and pour liquids, clean up spills with a sponge, sort laundry, put away folded clothes, and pour dry food for pets.

O When he is five: he can comb his hair, pack his lunch, make simple microwave meals, use a knife to slice cheese or fruit, make a peanut-butter-and-jelly sandwich, fold laundry, help grocery shop, and push the vacuum cleaner.

O When he is six to ten years old: he can walk the dog, pull weeds or plant flowers, operate the washer and dryer, make his bed, help prepare meals, and empty or load the dishwasher. Older boys may want to have a paper route, wash cars, or mow lawns to earn money.

Of course, he can learn to do these tasks only if you take time to train him and make room for him to practice. Remember, keep your standards realistic. It's also okay to have fun; making a game of work sometimes takes the sting out of it. It is more important for your son to learn new skills in an atmosphere of encouragement than to do tasks perfectly.

RESPONSIBILITY IN THE OLDER BOY

As your son matures he should take responsibility for more and more of his life. Keep in mind that your son is still a beginner; he will make mistakes and can learn valuable lessons from them if you remain calm and understanding.

A school-age boy can and should be responsible for his own homework (you can help, but he will learn only if he does the work), keeping track of sports equipment or other possessions, and personal care. You can make routine charts together to help him remember what must be done and when. As much as you can, teach skills, offer a reminder or two, and then step back and let your son learn from his choices and experiences. Painful as it may be, many people learn more from a mistake than they do from success.

Chores and Allowance

Among the issues that ignite family arguments, chores and allowance are high on the list. You probably believe that your son needs to help out with chores; you also may understand that he needs some money of his own, especially as he gets older and more independent. Should you pay him for doing chores? If so, how much? And if not, what should you do about giving him an allowance and expecting cooperation?

CHORE WARS

Chores are more than jobs you expect your son to do (moaning and whining all the way). Chores and family work are opportunities for your son to learn that he is a contributing member of the family, that he can help others, and that he has useful abilities and skills. Chores will also help him learn to plan ahead, follow through, and organize his time. Of course, chores can also become a power struggle as you try to make your son do his work.

Chores may be high on your list of priorities, but it is unlikely that your son shares your opinion. What normal ten-year-old would rather be inside cleaning his room than outside playing with friends? Let your son know that helping with chores is part of being a family, and then work together to make a plan.

When your son is old enough to help regularly with chores, consider having a family meeting to talk about each person's responsibilities. Start simple: It is easier to gain cooperation when neither you nor your son feels overwhelmed. Be sure to talk about when each task should be completed. You can create a family chore chart or other system to act as a reminder, but it is best to avoid stickers, money, and rewards. (More about that in a moment.)

You may find that your son is happy to cooperate when he has a voice in deciding on chores and schedules, which is why family meetings work so well. Your boy may hate dusting but be quite willing to vacuum or mow the lawn. Making a plan together (and reviewing it occasionally) will help you avoid needless arguments. Chores are a practical way for your son to learn how capable he really is.

ALLOWANCE

Parents want money and usually wish they had more of it, so it shouldn't surprise you to learn that children want money, too. Even young children need to learn how to handle money wisely. Many parents give their children an allowance, but allowances usually have lots of strings attached.

For instance, a boy may have to do all of his chores perfectly by the agreed-upon deadline to get his allowance (leading to heated arguments about whether a task was done "right" or "on time"). Or his grades might have to be acceptable. Perhaps he has to be respectful or practice the piano every day. Parents concoct complicated systems for tying a boy's allowance to his performance at school or at home. All too often, these systems collapse under their own weight.

Your boy needs to learn that there are some things he must do just because he is part of a family. (It's called making a contribution.) Sometimes, paying children to do chores teaches them to expect a material reward for everything they do; the reward, rather than the skills and attitudes to be learned, becomes the focus of the task.

Here is a way of dealing with chores and allowance that teaches cooperation, responsibility, and respect:

○ Offer your son an age-appropriate allowance. Consider the amount carefully—you want to teach him responsibility, not fund his video-game habit. Give him the allowance each week with no strings attached.

○ Do not allow borrowing against the allowance. If your son wants more money to buy something special, help him learn that he can save each week's allowance and will eventually have enough for his purchase.

○ Allow your son to decide what to do with his money. You can take time to teach him about saving, giving to charity, or spending, but he will learn best from his own experience. (You can help by asking "what" and "how" questions, such as, "What would have happened if you had saved your money instead of spending it?")

○ Make chores a separate issue from allowance. Your boy has chores because he is part of the family; he receives an allowance because he needs to have money of his own. You can use family meetings to discuss chores and money management.

O Avoid rescuing your son if he makes poor choices about money. Instead of handing out money, help him make a plan for solving his problem (such as doing extra tasks like babysitting or yard work to pay what he owes). Remember, the skills your son learns are more important than the toy he wants.

You will need to sit down with your son from time to time to make sure your agreements about chores and allowance are working well for both of you. Your son may never love chores, but he can learn important skills by doing them.

The Art of Managing Money

When he has it, money may just burn a hole in your little boy's pocket. There are games to rent, candy and toys to buy, and interesting stuff to collect. Your son may no sooner have a few quarters in his hand than he begs to be driven to the store. Not surprisingly, your son does not yet know how to handle money; many adults these days struggle, too. In fact, credit card debt is now at an all-time high, while retirement savings are at an all-time low. Managing money isn't a skill that always comes naturally, and just like with any behavior, there may be an underlying reason why your son handles money a certain way.

TEACHING OPPORTUNITIES
Managing money and keeping a budget are often learned through trial and error—especially error. Who hasn't suffered a bout of buyer's remorse or credit card anxiety at least once?

KIND AND FIRM
Opportunities to teach your son about money abound in daily life. A trip to the grocery store, shopping for school clothes, or talking about college can

all be moments to help your son learn to make and keep a budget. Children do not automatically understand where money comes from and how difficult it is to earn. After all, they see parents going to the ATM and walking away with a handful of bills; money must be easy to come by!

When your son is old enough, take him with you to the bank and open a savings account in his name. You can give him the savings book to keep in a special place. When your son receives birthday or other special money, he may choose to deposit some or all of it in his account.

One of the best ways to teach your son to handle money wisely is to do so yourself. Talk to him about saving, spending, and debit or credit cards. Help him understand the difference between wants and needs and how to plan for both. While your son should never be asked to make important financial decisions, you can help him understand how money is managed in your family.

Be aware that many credit card companies target high school and college students, offering credit card accounts with low limits to "help your student establish good credit." Young adults often misuse these cards, running up debts they cannot pay. Be wary of credit card offers; teach your son the risks of credit.

DELAYED GRATIFICATION

We live in a "fast-food" culture; most of us prefer to get what we want when we want it. One of the hidden pitfalls of pampering children is that they may grow up expecting to receive the things they want immediately—and be seriously unhappy when these things do not materialize as ordered. It is unlikely that your son's future boss, college professors, drill sergeant, or spouse will be as generous as you are.

Before you rush out to buy your son the latest cool toy or clothing brand, think about what he is learning. In the future there will be many times when he needs to earn money, save, wait a while, or appreciate what he has, so it's important to let him work a bit now for what he wants.

> Many children don't take care of their possessions because they have been given too much and do not appreciate what they have. Ultimately, a strong family bond has more value than physical possessions, but this is a concept that must be modeled. Let your son know that if he breaks or loses something that it is not the end of the world, but he must help replace it. Be kind and firm; focus on teaching responsibility and gratitude.

Learning on the Job

By the time they turn sixteen, most boys decide that they want to get a job. New cars, date money, and fashionable clothing beckon, and work can't be that hard—can it? A job is a valuable way for boys to learn responsibility, real-world skills, and money management. On the other hand, a job can also take time away from schoolwork, athletics, and other important activities. When is your son mature enough to handle a job?

> As your son enters the adult world, teach him the value of ethics. Examples of unethical behavior are everywhere these days: Corporate misconduct, performance-enhancing drug scandals, and political events may make it appear that honesty, responsibility, and principles don't matter—getting ahead does. Teach your son (and model) the values you want him to carry into his workplace and his adult life.

Most employers will not hire a boy until he is sixteen; many also require a valid driver's license. While some employers will limit a teen's hours to ensure he does well in school, others expect long hours and weekend work in return for minimum wage. Whether or not to get a job is a decision you and your son should make together. Let your son know what your priorities are. For instance, you might agree that he must maintain a certain grade point average in order to continue working.

You should also explore what your son should do with the money he earns. Can he spend all of it, or should he begin saving some for college or a car of his own? Be sure he makes time for activities he enjoys, getting adequate sleep (nine to ten hours each night for teenagers), and spending time with friends and family. Your son may need your help as he learns to balance the demands of his employer, his teachers, and his family.

Work can help a boy learn to show up on time, follow instructions, and do his best. Create regular opportunities to talk together about job skills, what he is learning, and ways to make his job part of a healthy and successful life.

Manners and Respect

If you spend much time around groups of young people, you may notice that behavior and manners have changed a bit from the time when you were young. Language is rougher; while many teens are courteous and kind, others no longer offer automatic respect to their elders. Adults often comment that they would never have dared behave the way their children do, but then again, times have changed. Or have they?

THE VALUE OF RESPECT

All relationships that work, whether in a family, at school, or in the workplace, are built on understanding and mutual respect. In a perfect world, children learn about respect because they see it modeled for them every day. When parents treat each other, themselves, and their children with respect, children learn to do the same. In reality, however, respect can be a rare commodity. And like other attitudes and character qualities, respect must be conscientiously taught.

Much of the music and entertainment that appeals to children and teens is inherently disrespectful. Sitcom families and cartoon kids speak disrespectfully, and everyone laughs; it's not all that shocking that, in turn, real children try the same approach. Nevertheless, respect is a quality that is still highly valued. It becomes especially important when your son leaves your home and must get along with other adults in order to build a successful, independent life.

Ensure that respect is a fundamental part of your family life. Talk about respect often; be sure that your son has the opportunity to see it in action. Your son will learn far more when you can practice dignity and respect as a family.

MANNERS AND PROFANITY

Most parents are delighted and proud when their little boy politely says "please," "thank you," and "excuse me." Parents are a bit less delighted when the preschool years pass and children seem to shed their manners along with their diapers. If you believe that manners and common courtesy are important, be sure you continue to model and teach them in your family. Your son will make his own decisions about whether to practice courtesy on his own, but he is far more likely to do so if you show him how.

Profanity is sometimes a challenge for parents of boys, especially during the teen years. Boys often view cursing and rough language, like other risky behavior, as traits of masculinity. They feel manly and sophisticated when they let loose with a barrage of four-letter words. You might tell your son that you know he may curse with his friends, but that you would prefer not to hear that language—and you don't want him speaking that way to teachers or other adults. This lesson will be much easier to teach, of course, if you refrain from using profanity yourself.

Practice Self-Reliance

Letting go is hard. Not only must parents step aside and make room for a boy to build his own life, but they must also trust that boy—still young and unskilled—to go out into the world and make good decisions. The risks are very real, and parents often cling too long and too hard in an effort to prevent a beloved son from making mistakes.

But your job as a conscious parent is to prepare your son for life away from you. Self-reliance, confidence, and independence are qualities that can only be obtained in the real world. Your son will learn to stand on his own two feet only if you allow him to practice. If you begin when he is young, he can learn self-reliance in a safe environment, before the risks become too great.

Just in case you were wondering, here's a news flash: Your son, no matter how wonderful, loving, and talented, will not be perfect. And that is okay. All he needs to be is good enough—good enough in his relationships, his work, and his ability to solve problems.

Your son will have the courage to tackle new challenges—work, relationships, college, or whatever else lies ahead—when you build a solid relationship, offer encouragement and teaching, and then have faith in his ability to manage his life. Taking time to say, "I have faith in you; I believe you can succeed" can make all the difference in the world to a boy just setting out on his own.

Throughout the years you spend together, there will be moments for you to step in and help and moments when you must step back. As your son enters the outside world, you can let him go, knowing that he has the ability to learn, grow, and succeed.

Important Points to Consider

Teaching your son to survive and thrive as an adult is one of your most important responsibilities as a conscious parent. Keep these considerations in mind:

O Involving your son in household tasks from a young age can build his self-esteem and build his life skills.

- Chores and allowance should be age-appropriate and the two topics should remain separate.

- Modeling respect can build respectful characteristics in your son.

- As difficult as it may be to let go, building his own life and interests is an important part of your son's development.

 **CHAPTER 15**

Nontraditional Family Dynamics

A wise person once said that a family is any circle of people who love each other. You can make sure that your son always has a loving, connected family regardless of how it meets with the traditional family model of long ago. One of the best ways to help your son through difficult events like divorce or remarriage is to encourage him to identify his emotions and talk about them. When he does talk, be accepting of these emotions and try not to internalize them or take them personally. It is possible and probable that parents and sons alike can thrive in a different family dynamic.

The Effect of Divorce on Boys

Divorce is a loss for everyone in the family. You will grieve, and so will your son. But you can also help each other stay connected. Don't try to fix your son's feelings; you cannot do that, no matter how much you love him. But you can offer understanding, encouragement, and support.

THE TRUTH ABOUT DIVORCE

In an ideal world, a boy lives with his mother and his father, experiences a sense of belonging and significance, and learns to be capable and competent as he grows up. (Obviously, even boys with married parents do not always experience this ideal situation!) When parents no longer live together, life for a boy becomes more complicated, but it need not be impossible.

Many people believe that children of divorced parents will never have healthy marriages or relationships themselves. Not true! A University of Michigan study of more than 6,000 adults found that 43 percent of the adult children of divorced parents were happily married—about the same percentage as those who grew up in two-parent homes.

There are indeed risks associated with having divorced or separated parents:

O Boys are more likely to react to divorce with anger, academic problems, truancy, or aggressive behavior than girls, who may try to please adults by suppressing feelings.

O Boys are more likely to suffer from depression when the father leaves the home, especially when a boy is not able to spend time with him consistently.

- Boys may also lose connection with a mother because she must work longer hours to provide for the family and keep a home running.

- Boys may assume blame for the breakup of a family.

It is worth noting that many of the negative effects of divorce have to do with economics. Men are far more likely than women to maintain their standard of living after a divorce, while women (who still tend to have custody of children) find that their economic level falls significantly. Moving to neighborhoods and schools that are less safe and stable may account for some of the problems boys have in the aftermath of a divorce. It is critically important that fathers continue to offer emotional and financial support to their sons after divorce.

ENCOURAGE EMOTIONAL AWARENESS

Boys often mask their emotions in order to appear manly. They may want to protect their parents and may refuse to talk about their own pain, grief, and worry, or they may act out their feelings by misbehaving. One of the best ways to help your son through difficult times is to encourage him to identify his emotions and to talk about them. When he does talk, be accepting of these emotions. Let him know that no matter how tired or anxious you may be, you always have time to listen to him.

Your attitude is also an important factor in how your son adjusts to divorce. If you consider yourself a victim or look for someone to blame, your son will mirror your beliefs. If you face your challenges, seek healing and help for yourself, and do your best to move into a new life, your son will learn from you.

Co-Parenting

For a child, having two parents in separate homes is just plain complicated. For instance, what should he do when he has homework and the computer is at Mom's? What happens when he has a baseball game and his equipment bag is at Dad's? What if Mom lets him watch television but

Dad won't—or vice versa? And what if he has to do chores at two separate homes? Now, how fair is that?

Co-parenting is difficult for parents, too. After all, if it had been easy to get along with your son's other parent, you might still be together. Still, with some thought (and perhaps some outside help), you should be able to manage logistics, money, and shared custody in a way that works for everyone.

WHAT CHILDREN NEED

Your son needs the freedom to love and communicate with both of his parents. It is never helpful to trash-talk your ex-partner, regardless of what he or she has done. Remember, that person is a part of your son. You can give a simple account of the facts without including harsh personal criticism or accusations. Be sure your son understands that divorce is an adult decision: It is *never* a child's fault, even though many children do feel responsible.

Moving between two homes can be complicated for all sorts of reasons. Children do best (as do adults) when there is respect, structure, and consistency. Many experts suggest creating a parenting plan to outline the details of shared custody, visits, education, and all the other issues parents must face. You may write this document yourselves, although some parents find it easier to work with a mediator or other professional. In *Positive Discipline for Single Parents*, Jane Nelsen, EdD, Cheryl Erwin, MA, and Carol Delzer, MA, JD, suggest including the following issues in a parenting plan:

O **Visitation schedules:** Where will children be for weekends, midweek visits, summers, holidays, and special events?

O **Custody:** Who has legal and/or physical custody?

O **Responsibility:** Who will make which decisions? Can stepparents participate?

O **Education:** What's your plan for school decisions, expenses, and college?

- **Medical and dental care and insurance:** Who will pay premiums and copayments? Who will carry a child on his or her policy?

- **Other insurance:** Who holds life insurance or auto insurance for teens?

- **Mental health care:** Who decides about counseling? Who has access to information?

- **Childcare:** Who selects childcare? Be sure to include pick-up and drop-off instructions.

- **Parenting education:** Attending a parenting class can be helpful to both parents. Who will decide when, where, and from whom to take parenting classes? Will you attend together or separately?

- **Religious training:** What about church attendance or Hebrew school?

- **Contact with extended family:** How will you handle visits with grandparents, siblings, and cousins?

- **Moving:** Can either parent move out of town and take the children?

- **Activities:** Who will pay for sports, dance, music, and so on? Who will attend?

- **Transportation:** How will you handle transportation to and from activities and homes?

- **Access to school and other records:** Who has it?

- **Tax consequences:** Who gets the deduction?

- **Schedule changes:** How will you deal with things such as business travel and emergencies?

It is also wise to have a backup plan for resolving disagreements and unexpected problems. It may be helpful to view co-parenting your son as a sort of business relationship; you don't have to like each other to do a good job. Respect, courtesy, and cooperation are essential. You may not like your ex-partner, but your son will be happier and healthier when you can work together to ease transitions, create structure, and share information.

AVOID THE TUG OF WAR

Children universally hate being in the middle of warring parents. Some parents treat children like the rope in a tug of war, pulling and yanking in an effort to win. This sort of behavior will only hurt your son.

Do your best to handle adult matters yourself; let your son remain a child. Children should never be asked to resolve money issues or ask a parent for child support. They should never be expected to provide information about one parent's behavior to the other parent. ("Does your dad have a girlfriend? Does she spend the night?") If you have reason to suspect that your son is being mistreated or neglected at his other parent's home, you will have to take action. Otherwise, offer respect and allow your son to build his own relationship with his other parent. Focus on providing your son with one home that is filled with love, laughter, and trust.

Being Mom and Dad

Being a single parent can feel overwhelming, and it's okay if you feel that way. There often isn't enough time or money to go around, and finding a moment to take a shower or run to the grocery store without children in tow can be impossible. But life in a single-parent home can also be rewarding. You decide how your home will run; you set the tone of your relationship with your son.

LIFE IN A SINGLE-PARENT HOME

Single parents sometimes struggle to balance all the responsibilities they carry. And many worry that a growing boy needs a full-time mother and father. Is one parent really enough?

It is unlikely that you can simultaneously fill both the roles of good mother and good father, no matter how hard you try. And in truth, your son does not need you to single-handedly be both parents. Coaches, neighbors, friends, and other family members can all provide support, teaching, and fun (as well as a respite for you from full-time parenting). Don't hesitate to ask for help when you need it. A skilled therapist, a single-parenting class, or a support group may provide ideas and encouragement.

As you have throughout your conscious parenting journey, focus on building a loving and consistent connection with your son; be sure that you stay tuned in and find time to talk and listen uninterrupted on a regular basis. One good enough parent in your home is all your son truly needs.

Single mothers can raise sons to be happy, capable adults, but it helps to pay attention to your own attitudes toward men. Be sure that any anger or resentment you feel toward your son's father does not spill over onto him. Boys are particularly sensitive to their mothers' attitudes toward men in general and their dads in particular.

KEEPING YOUR BALANCE

Part of being a successful single parent is learning to take care of yourself. You can and should make time for activities and relationships you enjoy. You may need to learn some new skills: Single parenting requires that you learn to manage money wisely, organize time efficiently, and provide kind, firm discipline.

Regular family meetings will help you and your son solve problems together. Believe it or not, life in a single-parent home presents children with real opportunities to learn skills, make a contribution, and feel genuine belonging. Choose your priorities (and battles) carefully; there simply isn't enough time to deal with every issue every day. Be sure you spend your time and energy on the things that really matter.

Building Healthy Stepfamilies

Most of the adults who experience a divorce eventually remarry, and the resulting stepfamilies often create interesting combinations of "yours, mine, and ours." Some children in a stepfamily may go back and forth between parents' homes at varying times, while others live there full-time. Chores, rooms, space, time, and affection all can generate challenges (and arguments). It's also true that stepfamilies can be filled with love, joy, and hope.

DIVIDED LOYALTIES

You may believe that when you remarry, it is just a matter of time before you live happily ever after. Unfortunately, expecting adults and children who do not share blood or history to love each other immediately can create disappointment and conflict.

Remarriage inspires some interesting questions about love and loyalty. Most stepparents will hear the dreaded phrase "You're not my real dad (or mom)" at some point in their lives. Conflict with stepparents seems to be part of our cultural heritage; after all, look at how many myths and fairy tales feature a wicked stepmother or a cruel stepfather! Unraveling loyalties—the bonds between parents and children—can be one of the most difficult tasks in building a healthy stepfamily.

It is usually wise for a boy's birth parent to take the lead in providing discipline and setting limits. If your son does not yet respect or accept your new partner, he may be less likely to cooperate. Work together to set limits; focus on building connections. Trust and respect often develop with familiarity.

Your son will need time to accept your new partner and to figure out that person's place in his life. You cannot control or dictate your son's feelings, but you can encourage appropriate behavior. Stepparents and other adult partners can become trusted friends, mentors, and confidants, even though they are not birth parents. Be patient, offer understanding, and follow through with kind, firm discipline.

WORKING WITH YOUR NEW PARTNER

Loyalty can be a problem not just between families but also within them. It is natural for a parent to favor his or her own child and to feel less of a connection with a partner's child, but this situation can cause real hurt to everyone. It may seem tempting or even necessary to protect your son from your new partner; you may believe your parenting skills are superior and try to help your new stepchildren. Unfortunately, if you assume authority too quickly, resentment may follow.

When you understand the importance of belonging and significance and focus on creating real connection among family members, working together to set limits and follow through becomes much easier. Regular family meetings will help everyone focus on finding solutions to problems and will help new family members get to know each other better.

Experts report that it takes an average of two to seven years for most stepfamilies to settle into comfortable rhythms and routines. Your stepfamily will not feel like your original family, but that's okay. Flexibility and patience are essential in building a stepfamily.

Few adults agree completely about parenting, no matter how much they love one another. You and your new partner will need to decide together how you will approach raising your shared children. A good parenting class or a few sessions with a counselor may be a wise investment and may save you unnecessary conflict and stress.

Growing Up Too Soon

Couples usually marry with hope, optimism, and confidence; certainly no one expects to get divorced one day. Yet marriages end, for all sorts of reasons, and parents and their children must go on to find new ways of living together. The challenges of life in a different sort of family can pressure a boy to grow up too soon. Sometimes, too, a parent may unintentionally force a boy to become a little man.

SINGLE MOTHERS AND SONS

Being the single parent of a child whose gender is different from your own can present unexpected problems. Single dads often struggle to understand the development and moods of daughters (let alone fashion and acceptable hairstyles); single mothers do not always intuitively understand the needs of their sons. Even the simplest things can be dilemmas. For instance, if you're a single mom with a seven-year-old son who is too old to enter the ladies' restroom, do you let him go to the men's room alone?

In *Real Boys*, William Pollack, PhD, quotes a study of 648 children, eight years after their parents' divorces. It found that boys living with single mothers were five times more likely to suffer from a major depressive disorder than girls living with single mothers. Boys living with single mothers were also more at risk than boys who had a consistent relationship with an adult male relative or friend.

A 1998 study by Ohio State University found that single fathers are no better at discipline than single mothers. If you are a single mother raising a son, it is important that you learn solid parenting skills and give some thought to your long-term goals. You can raise a contented son, even without the help of a live-in man.

Many successful, healthy men have been raised by single mothers. Still, boys living with single moms sometimes feel they must assume the responsibilities of their missing fathers. Sometimes, too, a mother expects her son to become the new man of the house.

ESTABLISHING HEALTHY BOUNDARIES

There is nothing wrong with expecting a son to cooperate with the work of keeping a home running smoothly. Expecting a boy to do a man's job, however, sets him up for failure. Your son, no matter how loving and mature, lacks the skills to be your partner, and while you can invite his suggestions, you must make the major decisions. There should never be any doubt about who the parent really is. It is not your son's job to shoulder your emotional burdens or to worry about the family finances—although he may do so without being asked.

You can and should tell your son, no matter how old he is, that you are the parent and it is your job to take care of him. You can also let him know that you do appreciate his help and support. If you experience depression or anxiety, don't hesitate to get help for yourself; never expect your son to take care of you.

You may be best able to truly love and enjoy your boy when the boundaries between you are clear, reasonable, and respectful. Take time to nurture yourself and enjoy your life and set your son free to enjoy being young.

Important Points to Consider

Divorce, single parents, and stepfamilies are common realities in today's world. If you find yourself in one of these situations, it is more important than ever to be a conscious parent to your son. These events will most certainly affect him, but how you approach them can go a long way in how he adjusts. Be available for your son to express his feelings about the situation, treat your former partner with a respect your son can model, and let your son enjoy being a kid. The following are some points to keep in mind:

O Divorce can have a profound impact on the life of a boy. Many boys feel the need to take on a caregiver role during a divorce. Encourage open communication and strong support from all adults in his life during this process.

O Modeling respectful and appropriate behavior is especially important after divorce. Treat your ex-partner with respect and keep open communication with him or her about matters involving your son. Treat the relationship as a business arrangement if need be.

O It is important to stay closely connected with your son before, during, and after a divorce.

O Single parents can be just as effective as dual-parent families. There are inherent challenges to being both mom and dad to your son, but you are also modeling resilience, discipline, and determination.

 **CHAPTER 16**

Moving Toward Independence

Letting go is a process that begins when your son is born. You must let go so that he can learn to feed himself, walk, and run. If you have worked together at letting go throughout his childhood, you and your son will be ready when it's time for him to begin life on his own. One of the paradoxes of raising a child is that when you do your job as a parent well, your child will leave you. Launching a son toward an independent life is more difficult than many parents expect.

Preparing Him for Independence

As long as your son lives under your roof, you are present to watch over him, teach him skills, and set limits on his behavior. Once your son moves out on his own, however, there is no watchful parent in the next room to make sure everything goes well. By the time your son leaves home, he will need to know how to manage his life effectively, make good decisions, and take care of himself.

The law says that a boy becomes a legal adult at the age of eighteen (whether or not he's fully mature); he can sign agreements and take on other adult responsibilities and obligations. This does not necessarily mean that he is ready for all of the responsibilities of adulthood. In fact, many eighteen-year-olds are still developing both physically and emotionally. Through your own interaction with your son, you are the best person to judge his level of maturity and some rules may still need to be abided by, especially if your son is still living in your home.

Chances are good that your son will not realize how much you have done for him until he needs to do it for himself. Beyond the daily necessities of food, clean clothes, and a comfortable place to live, he will discover the realities of medical and dental expenses, insurance payments, bank accounts, and income tax. Your son must manage his education or career. And he must know how to keep himself physically and emotionally healthy.

Teaching Life Skills

You may think you've heard all there is to hear about the importance of life skills, but the concept takes on a new urgency when your son announces that he's ready to move out. It becomes even more urgent the first time he calls you to announce he's run out of money, forgotten to put oil in his car, or clogged the plumbing of his new home.

If your son is joining the military or moving out to live in a college dormitory, some (if not all) of his daily decisions will be made for him. If he plans to live in a house or apartment, either alone or with roommates, he probably will need to have a few new skills under his belt.

Teenagers and young adults often resist parents' direct efforts to teach skills, usually because the lessons sound too much like lectures. You may find it helpful to sit down and make your own list of the skills your son will need once he is no longer living at home. (It's even better to do this when your son is fifteen or sixteen and you have a few years to work on it!) Ask yourself whether your son can handle the following tasks:

- Read care instructions on clothing and wash and dry them properly.

- Iron a shirt and slacks.

- Sew on a button and mend a seam.

- Compare prices, quantity, and quality when grocery shopping.

- Prepare at least six nutritious meals from scratch.

- Operate and maintain common household appliances.

- Check the oil and tire pressure on an automobile.

- Decide what to do in case of illness or a medical emergency.

- Locate a doctor or dentist.

- Balance a bank checkbook or access an online statement to manage his account.

- Prepare a resume, fill out a job application, and conduct a successful job interview.

- Understand a lease or legal agreement.

- Pay utility bills, credit card bills, and rent in a timely manner.

- File a claim for medical or automobile insurance.

- Keep records for income tax and file a return on time.

You can teach these skills to your son by inviting him to work with you as you do them. Or you can begin putting together a notebook of suggestions and information that he can refer to once he has moved out. You can include favorite family recipes, the names of doctors and dentists, family addresses and phone numbers, and other information you believe will be helpful.

Be cautious about doling out money once your son has moved out. Take some time to reflect: If you feel like you're being manipulated, you are. You can be both kind and firm as you allow your son to experience the results of his own budgeting (or lack thereof). Instead of rescuing, you can help him plan for coming expenses.

Take some time to consider whether your home will be open for drop-in meals, laundry service, or television viewing. Whether you welcome unexpected visits from your son or find them to be a nuisance will depend on his intentions. Always keep in mind the lessons you want your son to learn; be sure your actions encourage him to develop self-reliance, confidence, and respect. Coddling your son and cleaning up his messes may seem loving in the moment, but you will not be teaching him to make it on his own.

Becoming a Mentor

It's been said that you become an adult everywhere but in your old home, and there's some truth to the saying. All too often, parents find it impossible to let grown children handle their own lives, dispensing advice on everything from clothing to romance to careers.

When your son is young, you are responsible for his physical care, health, and safety. Sometimes managing the details of a boy's life becomes such a habit that parents fail to let go when they should. One of the best ways to create power struggles with a young adult is to continue running his life for him when he is convinced that he's ready to do it himself.

Letting go of your son does not mean abandoning or ignoring him. You can and should continue to participate in his life, but the way you do so must change. It may help you to think of your new role as that of a mentor or coach, instead of an active parent. You are there to offer support, encouragement, and, occasionally, active intervention. But it is usually wise to wait until you're invited before riding to the rescue.

Here are some phrases mentor parents should keep handy:

O Would you like my help?

O Do you want to hear a suggestion?

O What ideas do you have for solving that problem?

O Do you want to know what I think?

O Let me know if you need me.

Becoming a mentor means being connected and concerned but not overbearing or controlling. Your son is far more likely to welcome your participation in his life when you encourage his independence and celebrate his success.

When Your Son Returns Home

Young men usually leave home with high hopes. They leave for an education, a new job, or a promising new relationship. Sometimes, though, the world is not kind to them. It's hard to earn enough money for rent and expenses, and sometimes relationships with friends, roommates, or partners don't work out as planned. The college your son always dreamed of may be a disappointment; he may even flunk out. Sometimes young adults want to move back home. In fact, some young men move in and out several times before they acquire the confidence and skills they need to live successfully on their own.

BUNGEE FAMILIES

Most parents in a recent study reported that they expected their children to move out and become independent by the age of twenty-five. However, young adults are marrying and starting families of their own later in life now than ever before, at about age twenty-six for women and twenty-eight for men. In addition, many young adults report enjoying closer connections with their parents.

Writer and therapist Martha Straus, PhD, calls these closely connected families "bungee families." According to Straus, 25 million young adults between the ages of eighteen and thirty-four live with their parents, and 65 percent of college graduates move home for a year or two. Is it necessarily a bad thing if your adult son wants to return home? No—as long as you can agree on your expectations and obligations.

Several studies have concluded that the best predictor of positive academic and social outcomes at age twenty is "consistent, high-quality relationships" with parents. Those relationships should stay strong well into early adulthood.

No matter how much you love your son, it can be disappointing (and exhausting) when he becomes a full-time boarder. There are times when it makes sense for a young man to return home for a while; you may be more than happy to offer him refuge while he regroups and figures out what to do next. Keep in mind, however, that your relationship has changed: He is now an adult and you no longer owe him a place to live. Discussing the terms of your new relationship in advance will save everyone some heartache.

You have the right to set limits in your own home. If your adult son moves back in, be sure you reach an understanding about the following issues:

- How long will he be welcome to stay?

- Do you expect him to pay rent or contribute money toward groceries and other expenses?

- Think twice about providing special services. Who will be responsible for laundry, meals, and household chores?

- Can your son entertain overnight guests in his room? Do you expect him to return home by a specific time?

- How will you handle alcohol or drug use?

- Will you give your son money or assume responsibility for his bills?

You will need to recognize that an adult son operates by different rules than the little boy you once raised. For instance, it may be unrealistic to set a curfew; many young adults are just beginning the evening when parents are going to bed.

An honest discussion about house rules will help you agree on a plan that works for everyone. For instance, you may decide to give up the idea of a curfew and, instead, ask your son to be quiet and courteous if he returns to the house in the wee hours of the morning.

Adjusting to the Empty Nest

When children are young, home is a busy place. There always seems to be something to do and somewhere to go; you may long for peace and quiet and wonder what it feels like to be bored. Then your children move out and suddenly home feels completely different. The fledglings have flown, and the nest is empty.

There are some unexpected benefits to having an empty nest. Here are some you may not have thought of:

- It's quiet. The phone doesn't ring as often, and there is no more loud music—unless you're playing it yourself.

- The gas tank in your car stays full much longer.

- Food stays in the refrigerator, and the grocery bill goes down.

- You can buy things for yourself when you go shopping.

- The computer, telephone, and television are yours to control.

- The house stays clean, and there is far less laundry to do.

- You can be spontaneous: You can go out to dinner at the last minute, go dancing, or wander through the house naked.

Sometimes, though, having an empty nest hurts. The quiet can be either soothing or depressing. If you have enjoyed a close relationship with your son, you will undoubtedly miss his company, his laughter, and his stories about his day. You may find that you and your partner have focused your energy so completely on your son that you have little connection with each other.

Couples often find the time following a child's departure from home to be one of the most challenging in their relationship. In fact, the empty-nest period is one of the most common times for couples to separate or divorce, even when they have been married for decades. Be sure to make your relationship with your partner a priority as your son approaches maturity; take time to nurture intimacy and enjoy each other.

EMPTY-NEST SYNDROME

The parents most likely to struggle with grief and a sense of loss—what is commonly called the empty-nest syndrome—are those who have been overly involved with their children. If raising your son has been the central focus of your life for two or more decades, you may find it difficult to fill the empty hours once he leaves.

Many parents, however, find that the period following their children's departure is both rewarding and enjoyable. Because so many mothers work outside the home today, women are more likely to feel a continued sense of purpose and to have friends and activities.

Some research suggests that fathers may be the ones who have the hardest time when children leave. While an associate professor of psychology at Wheaton College, Helen DeVries, PhD, studied the effects of an empty nest on men and women. She found that even stay-at-home moms tended to look forward to the day their children left home and had made plans to fill their time. Fathers, on the other hand, often failed to anticipate the emotional impact of having a child leave and were more likely to feel regret over lost opportunities to spend time with their children.

WHAT TO DO NEXT

Raising a boy takes years of energy, care, and patience. When he goes off to experience the world, you have the opportunity to focus all of that energy on other things. You will never stop loving or caring for your son, but you can find ways to make these years of your life enjoyable and rewarding. If you haven't considered what you will do when your son leaves home, here are some suggestions:

○ Explore interests you haven't had time to pursue. You might want to learn a new type of cooking, plant a garden, or learn to fly an airplane.

○ Return to school or get a graduate degree. You have years of accumulated wisdom and experience; it may be worthwhile to put them to use.

○ Travel.

○ Plan activities, trips, and events with your partner. Invest in your adult relationships.

○ Do volunteer work.

○ Start a business. You may turn a lifelong interest in interior decorating into a successful consulting business or cater private parties and other events.

○ Improve your health and fitness. You can take a yoga class, hike with the Sierra Club, or ride a bicycle.

You can be supportive of your son while you devote time and energy to your own needs. Demonstrating initiative, self-respect, and enthusiasm may encourage your son to do the same.

Staying Connected to Your Son

Wherever your son goes, it will remain important to both of you to stay connected and involved in each other's lives. While he may no longer need your full-time care and supervision (or at least, so you hope), most adult sons continue to value their parents' love, wisdom, and support as they build their own lives and families.

The home you have shared with your son will provide him with roots for the rest of his life; your encouragement as he flies and experiences life gives him wings. No matter where your son goes, you can keep the connection between you strong and vital. If you are not already computer literate, take time to learn how to send and receive e-mail. Texting and social networking sites can also be excellent ways to stay in regular contact with each other. Digital photography will enable you to share pictures and memories, and old-fashioned cards and letters are always welcome. Time never stands still, but the future can hold wonderful times for you and your son.

Important Points to Consider

Letting go is difficult for most parents. After years of caring for your son and working hard to build strong bonds with him it can be sad when he goes forth into the world to start his own life. Even though you may rationally understand that this was your job as a parent—to prepare him for his own independent life—it can still be difficult to let your baby go. Here are some points to keep in mind:

- Preparing your son for adulthood is a process that begins at birth. You taught him the independence he needs in so many ways throughout his life, and this is the culmination of those lessons.

- Actively teaching your son valuable life skills will better prepare him to thrive as an adult. Though it can feel like you are doing your son a loving service by taking care of things for him, you are actually teaching him dependence. Give your son the space to make mistakes so he can learn and grow from them.

○ If your son returns home to live with you for whatever reason, it is important to establish rules and limits so that you can preserve your relationship without new resentments getting in the way. Limits will help you both retain your independence.

○ Healthy connection and support generally continue throughout the adult years. Just because your son has left your home does not mean he is gone from your life. Since you have formed strong bonds with your son he will be forever connected to you, no matter how old he becomes.

 **CHAPTER 17**

Celebrate Your Son

As the years of hands-on conscious parenting come to a close, you will undoubtedly have moments of regret and worry, as well as wonderful memories of shared times. No parent is perfect; all parents make mistakes and errors in judgment. Most lose control and say or do things they regret from time to time. Your son will not be perfect, either. He has lessons still to learn, no matter how old he is. As your lives continue to weave in and out of each other, you will continue to learn, grow, and make mistakes. Chances are, though, that if you work at staying connected, your relationship will provide joy and learning for both of you.

Appreciate the Man Your
Son Has Become

If you are just beginning your journey as a parent with a little boy tumbling energetically around the house, you may find the idea of reading an entire novel or playing golf almost laughable. But believe it or not, eventually that day will come. The passing of time, along with the changes time brings, is inevitable for all of us, and one day your son will not need you to feed him, clothe him, or put him to bed.

When a boy is young, it is all but impossible to know who he will become. He is busy wrestling with language, operating his sometimes uncooperative arms and legs, and exploring the world around him. Gradually, though, as you listen and spend time together, the person he truly is begins to emerge.

WHO IS YOUR SON?

Boys rarely turn out to be exactly what their parents expected. Some things about your son will make you smile; some may be a little disappointing. You may have hoped for a professional athlete, a talented musician, or a successful businessman. You may be longing for grandchildren while your son travels the world, in no hurry whatsoever to settle down. Your son may have made a number of choices that you simply don't understand and don't like.

If you reflect back on your own childhood and young adulthood, you will probably discover that you have changed a great deal over the years. Life does that to people: We must adapt and learn from our experiences, and hopefully become wiser, stronger individuals. You may look at your boy and be filled with love and pride; you may shake your head and wonder if he (and you) will survive. Do remember, however, that your son's story is not fully written. He is a work in progress and will always need your faith, encouragement, and wisdom.

Changing Roles

Take a moment to reflect on your relationship with your own parents. How often did you talk to them after you left home? Were you glad to hear their voices on the telephone or did you try to hang up as quickly as possible?

When they came for a visit, were you sad or relieved when they left? Or did they never come at all? What sort of relationship do you wish you had with your own parents?

You will always be your son's parent. But the way you conduct your relationship once he has reached maturity must change. You may be convinced you know better than your son what he should do, where he should live, and perhaps, whom he should date or marry. And you may even be right. But just as your boy resisted your efforts to control him when he was three or fifteen, he is unlikely to welcome your unsolicited advice now. If you hang on too tightly or intrude too much, your son is likely to want distance rather than closeness.

Gifted children and teenagers, while intense about their activities, are just as likely to be mentally healthy and happy as their less gifted peers—unless they have overly demanding parents who focus only on success and achievement. Children with demanding parents may fear making mistakes; they cannot enjoy their accomplishments because they're constantly worrying about the next challenge.

As your son matures, your role becomes that of an encourager. You can guide and suggest, and if you've built a relationship of connection and respect over the years, your boy will welcome your suggestions (well, at least most of the time) as he travels toward real maturity.

In *I Don't Want to Talk about It*, Terrence Real defines maturity, in part, as "the experience of communion and giving." Real writes, "Service is the appropriate central organizing force of mature manhood. When the critical questions concern what one is going to get, a man is living in a boy's world. Beyond a certain point in a man's life, if he is to remain truly vital, he needs to be actively engaged in devotion to something other than his own success and happiness." Your son must find the purpose and meaning of his own life. Your job will be to stay close, cheer him on, and offer support when needed—not to do the work for him.

Believe in Your Son

No matter how old your son is—and regardless of whether or not he admits it—he craves your acceptance and your love. He wants you to be proud of him; he wants to know that he is good enough just as he is, even when you're encouraging him to try something new. One of the greatest gifts you can give your son is your faith in him and in his ability to make a success of his life.

As your son grows, you can talk with him about people he admires. Help him understand the importance of character; teach him to look beyond mere words, appearance, and material success to the value of a life well lived. He will have to decide for himself how to live, but you will know that you have taught him well.

Think for a moment about men you have known and respected. You may think of a family member, a favorite teacher, a political figure, or another dad on the block. Perhaps you admire a musician, an actor, or an artist. Now think for a moment about the qualities you respect in that person. What has made him successful? What things do you particularly admire?

You may discover that there are many ways of being a good man. Success, too, has many definitions. Not all successful, accomplished, and respected men are alike, and your son needs freedom and support to become the man he is intended to be. This is easy to say but sometimes difficult to put into practice—especially if your son's goals and values in life differ from your own.

All parents have dreams for their children. Eventually, though, all parents must release those children to live their own lives. You can let your son know that you believe in him, even when you may disagree with his choices. Knowing you have faith in him—that you believe in the person he is becoming—will carry your son through many challenges.

Traditions and Celebrations

Your bond with your son will always be important. Memories are the only part of the past that we get to keep. And for many families, the warmest memories are woven around family holidays, vacations, and special events. From your boy's first birthday celebration to his graduation from high school, the traditions and rituals you create together keep family connections alive.

Richard Bromfield, PhD, a researcher at Harvard Medical School, points out that childhood encompasses 6,570 days, four presidencies, 1.8 decades, and nearly 1 million minutes. It sounds like a lot of time, yet parents discover that it passes all too quickly. Take time to enjoy your son and to appreciate the present moment while he is still under your roof.

You may not realize that children often value these special celebrations as much as you do. Even when your adolescent son rolls his eyes and sighs deeply, he may still look forward to choosing his own dinner menu, eating it on the special family birthday plate, and finding the lucky sticker hidden under his chair.

Family traditions often are passed on from generation to generation; these rituals become sacred spaces in our otherwise hectic lives. Here are a few ideas to keep in mind about family celebrations:

○ **Nurture connection.** Regardless of your faith tradition, ethnic background, or history, make every effort to focus your celebrations and rituals on relationships rather than food, gifts, or other things that distract from the real meaning of the day.

○ **Talk with family members about what they value.** As your children grow and your family changes, your traditions may need to change as well. Check in with family members occasionally to see what they truly enjoy and appreciate.

- **Be flexible.** Your son may miss a holiday or two because of work or education, or he may want to invite a new friend to come home with him. Insisting on doing things the way you always have may discourage your son from participating.

- **Watch your stress level.** Your entire family is likely to enjoy celebrations more when you are relaxed and cheerful.

- **Invite contributions from family members.** Your son may one day want to host a holiday celebration at his own home, or he may make suggestions about food, rituals, or other activities. Welcoming new ideas will keep your traditions alive and strong.

- **Appreciate the moment.** Be sure you take time to breathe and to feel gratitude for the time you share with family—even if yours doesn't always resemble a Norman Rockwell painting.

As your son grows and matures, special times to celebrate and reconnect will become increasingly important to all of you. Take time to laugh and play; find ways to gather your family together even when distance separates you. The bonds of family love truly can grow stronger with the passage of time.

Ways to Stay in Touch

Everyone is busy. Parents work; children and teens have dozens of activities. Keeping the lines of communication open can be a challenge even when children are young. The process is even more complicated when they move away from home, but it is no less important.

As your son becomes increasingly independent, you can find many ways to convey love, interest, and encouragement, whether he still lives at home or has gone off on his own. Here are a few suggestions:

- **Become tech-savvy.** Learn to send text messages, e-mail, and other quick notes. Consider becoming "friends" on a social network such as Facebook. Receiving a "Hi, I'm thinking of you" message in the midst of a busy day can brighten many stressful situations.

- O **Send a letter or card.** Old-fashioned paper greetings are still wonderful, and they can be pinned up on a bulletin board or tucked away in a drawer for later.

- O **Make phone calls easy.** Consider getting a cell phone family plan to make staying in touch easier (and less expensive).

- O **Plan a visit.** Your son may not have the time or the money to travel home often and may appreciate a visit from you. Use your common sense; visits usually are more enjoyable when you can recognize that your son also has commitments and interests of his own.

- O **Send a care package.** If your son lives away from home, a box filled with food items, books, photographs, or small mementos may be deeply appreciated.

One of the paradoxes of raising a boy is that you may miss him most just as he's learning to love his freedom. It is tempting to call or visit often, but many young men perceive excess attention as intrusive. Making your son feel guilty for not needing you will not improve your relationship. Celebrate your son's ability to thrive on his own; respect his need for privacy and independence. Remember to practice simple courtesy. Your son is more likely to welcome calls and visits when you are sensitive to his needs.

Staying in touch with your son as he matures can be a balancing act. You must allow him space to stretch his wings while still letting him know that you care. Your inner wisdom and knowledge of your son will help you know when to stay close and when to take a step back and let him experience the world for himself.

Give Yourself Credit

You have learned about infants, toddlers, school-age boys, and teenagers. You have been inundated with tips, facts, tools, and suggestions. But one important thing has been left unsaid: None of this could have happened without you.

Parenting—the art of raising a child to capable, happy adulthood—is underappreciated by society. After all, plenty of people have kids, and every parent should be able to raise one competently. Shouldn't they? Truthfully, however, changes in society and in twenty-first-century families have made raising a boy to confident, successful maturity far more challenging than it has ever been before.

A job offers the sense that you have accomplished something worthwhile. You receive timely feedback, and you are paid for the work you do. Parenting, on the other hand, does not offer such immediate rewards. You must have faith in yourself and your children, and believe that one day your efforts will be worthwhile.

YOU'VE DONE YOUR BEST

Think for a moment about your most difficult moments as a parent. Most parents can acknowledge that there have been times when they struggled to be loving, patient, firm, and kind. There were undoubtedly times when you failed to do what you believed you should. And there have been moments when you did not know what to do next, or when you had to accept that you had made a mistake.

It may be helpful to know that being less than perfect simply makes you human. The good news is that perfection is not a requirement for being a good, conscious parent. You will never be perfect and neither will your son. Rather than blaming yourself for mistakes, failures, and errors in judgment, take a moment to give yourself credit for being there, for offering love and acceptance, and for doing the best you could in a difficult world to raise a capable, competent young man.

Doing the right thing always appears easy when you're reading about it in a book or watching one of the many television experts. But real life is different than books or television. Raising a son is a great deal harder when you must face the daily ups and downs of life with an active, curious boy and somehow make decisions that help him learn character and important life skills. You have undoubtedly done the best you could as you raised your son; no one can do better than their best.

USING YOUR JUDGMENT TO SHAPE A SON

When all is said and done, you must decide what matters most. Take a moment to review the list of character qualities you created for your son.

Has he achieved most of them? If you are like most families, there are both successes and failures scattered along the path. You have dreams and fears for your boy, and regardless of where he goes and what he accomplishes, you will never stop caring about him.

There are no guarantees in raising a son. He has wonderful strengths and some limitations; so do you. Learn to listen to your heart. The love you feel for your boy, your knowledge of the man he is becoming, and your own inner wisdom will guide you in knowing what to do.

Important Points to Consider

Congratulations! You've raised a happy, well-adjusted son. Sure, you've struggled and tripped a few times along the journey, and may have caused ruptures in your relationship with your son, but you took the steps to be honest and open with him, too. You've tried your best to rectify your mistakes, and you've always been there to listen to your son and focus on the issues that have mattered to him. Now, here is your boy, all grown up and independent—you've done a marvelous job. Here are some points to keep in mind as your son goes off into the world:

O Staying connected with your son is helpful for both of you. You've formed strong bonds with your boy, helped him grow, and become his mentor. Now, as he begins his own life, your being there for him when he needs advice, help through bad times, or just someone to celebrate life's joys with will be invaluable to both of you. It will let him know he always has someone there in his corner.

O Have faith in your son and the life he will create, and don't forget to give yourself credit for all the good work you have put into being a conscious, caring parent. You've both done a tremendous job.

Appendix A: Bibliography

Biederman, Jerry, and Lorin Biederman, eds. *Parent School: Simple Lessons from the Leading Experts on Being a Mom and Dad* (New York: M. Evans and Co., 2002).

Bromfield, Richard, PhD, and Cheryl Erwin, MA. *How to Turn Boys Into Men Without a Man Around the House: A Single Mother's Guide* (Roseville, CA: Prima, 2002).

Chess, Stella, MD, and Alexander Thomas, MD. *Know Your Child* (New York: Basic Books, 1987).

Colapinto, John. *As Nature Made Him: The Boy Who Was Raised As a Girl* (New York: HarperCollins, 2000).

Commission on Children at Risk. *Hardwired to Connect: The New Scientific Case for Authoritative Communities* (Institute for American Values, 2003).

Dreikurs, Rudolf, MD, with Vicki Soltz, RN. *Children: The Challenge* (New York: Plume Books, 1991).

Dweck, Carol S., PhD. *Mindset: The New Psychology of Success* (New York: Random House, 2006).

Frontline. *Inside the Teenage Brain* (PBS Video, Public Broadcasting Service, 2002).

Gilbert, Susan. *A Field Guide to Boys and Girls* (New York: HarperCollins, 2000).

Goleman, Daniel. *Social Intelligence: The New Science of Human Relationships* (New York: Bantam Dell, 2006).

Gopnik, Alison, PhD, Andrew N. Meltzoff, PhD, and Patricia K. Kuhl, PhD. *The Scientist in the Crib: What Early Learning Tells Us about the Mind* (New York: HarperCollins, 1999).

Hallowell, Edward M., MD, and John J. Ratey, MD. *Driven to Distraction: Recognizing and Coping with Attention Deficit Disorder from Childhood Through Adulthood* (New York: Touchstone, 1995).

Healy, Jane M., PhD. *Endangered Minds: Why Children Don't Think and What We Can Do about It* (New York: Touchstone, 1990).

Hersch, Patricia. *A Tribe Apart: A Journey Into the Heart of American Adolescence* (New York: Ballantine, 1998).

Kindlon, Dan, PhD, and Michael Thompson, PhD. *Raising Cain: Protecting the Emotional Life of Boys* (New York: Ballantine, 2000).

Kohn, Alfie. *Punished by Rewards: The Trouble with Gold Stars, Incentive Plans, A's, Praise, and Other Bribes* (Boston: Houghton Mifflin, 1993).

Nelsen, Jane, EdD. *Positive Discipline* (New York: Ballantine, 2006).

Nelsen, Jane, EdD, and Cheryl Erwin, MA. *Parents Who Love Too Much: How Good Parents Can Learn to Love More Wisely and Develop Children of Character* (Roseville, CA: Prima, 2000).

Nelsen, Jane, EdD, Cheryl Erwin, MA, and Carol Delzer, MA, JD. *Positive Discipline for Single Parents: Nurturing, Cooperation, Respect, and Joy in Your Single-Parent Family, Revised and Updated 2nd Edition* (New York: Three Rivers Press, 1999).

Nelsen, Jane, EdD, Cheryl Erwin, MA, and Roslyn Ann Duffy. *Positive Discipline: The First Three Years: From Infant to Toddler—Laying the Foundation for Raising a Capable, Confident Child, 2nd Edition* (New York: Three Rivers Press, 2007).

Nelsen, Jane, EdD, Cheryl Erwin, MA, and Roslyn Ann Duffy. *Positive Discipline for Preschoolers: For Their Early Years—Raising Children Who Are Responsible, Respectful, and Resourceful, 3rd Edition* (New York: Three Rivers Press, 2007).

Nelsen, Jane, EdD, Lynn Lott, MA, MFT, and H. Stephen Glenn. *Positive Discipline A–Z: 1001 Solutions to Everyday Parenting Problems, Revised 3rd Edition* (New York: Three Rivers Press, 2007).

Pollack, William, PhD. *Real Boys: Rescuing Our Sons from the Myths of Boyhood* (New York: Random House, 1998).

Real, Terrence. *I Don't Want to Talk about It: Overcoming the Secret Legacy of Male Depression* (New York: Fireside, 1997).

Ricci, Isolina, PhD. *Mom's House, Dad's House: Making Two Homes for Your Child, Revised Edition* (New York: Fireside, 1997).

Shannon, Alice. "Beloved Stranger: Temperament and the Elusive Concept and Normality," *Psychotherapy Networker*, May/June 2005, vol. 29, no. 3, p. 62.

Siegel, Daniel J., MD. *The Developing Mind: How Relationships and the Brain Interact to Shape Who We Are* (New York: Guilford, 1999).

Siegel, Daniel J., MD., and Mary Hartzell, MEd. *Parenting from the Inside Out: How a Deeper Self-Understanding Can Help You Raise Children Who Thrive* (New York: Jeremy P. Tarcher/Penguin, 2003).

Straus, Martha, PhD. "Bungee Families," *Psychotherapy Networker*, September/October 2009, vol. 33, no. 5, p. 30.

Appendix B: Additional Resources

These websites are intended for use as general resources and information only. You are your son's parent; use your good judgment and wisdom when assessing the ideas you encounter.

Parenting Resources

The Adverse Childhood Experiences (ACE) Study
www.cdc.gov/nccdphp/ACE

HelpGuide—Trusted Guide to Mental, Emotional, and Social Health
www.helpguide.org

National Fatherhood Initiative
www.fatherhood.org

Positive Discipline Association
www.positivediscipline.org

Psychology Today
www.psychologytoday.com

Tufts University Child & Family WebGuide
www.cfw.tufts.edu

Zero to Three
www.zerotothree.org

Education and Literacy

Guys Read
www.guysread.com

National Association for the Education of Young Children
www.naeyc.org

Media, Violence, and Culture

Common Sense Media
www.commonsensemedia.org

Parent Further
www.parentfurther.com

Talk with Your Kids
www.talkwithkids.org

Cyberbullying

Stop Cyberbullying
www.stopcyberbullying.org

Wired Safety
www.wiredsafety.org

Development and Health

Child Development Institute
www.childdevelopmentinfo.com

KidsHealth
www.kidshealth.org

The Mayo Clinic
www.mayoclinic.org

Index